Family Fun - Alabama

Exciting Adventures For The Whole Family

Discover America Press

Published by Discover America Press, 2024.

FAMILY FUN - ALABAMA

First edition. March 27, 2024.

ISBN: 979-8224384402

Written by Discover America Press.

Table of Contents

Alabama is a state filled with diverse attractions and activities that cater to families of all sizes and ages. From the beautiful beaches of the Gulf Coast to the historic cities and natural wonders inland, there's no shortage of exciting adventures waiting to be explored. This book is designed to help you plan the perfect family getaway in Alabama, with a focus on destinations that offer fun, education, and lasting memories for everyone.

Inside, you'll find a curated list of more than 50 family-friendly attractions across the state, divided into regions for easy navigation. Each entry includes a brief description of the destination, along with key information such as address, phone number, hours of operation, and admission prices. We've also included age-appropriate recommendations and tips to help you make the most of your visit.

To ensure a smooth and enjoyable experience, we strongly recommend calling ahead to verify hours of operation and admission prices, as these may be subject to change. Many attractions also offer special events, discounts, or seasonal programs that you won't want to miss.

In addition to the main attractions, we've included a bonus section featuring 25 fun and easy-to-play road trip games that will keep your family entertained and engaged during your travels. These games are suitable for various age groups and require minimal supplies, making them perfect for any journey.

Whether you're planning a day trip, a weekend getaway, or a longer vacation, this book is your go-to guide for family fun in Alabama. So, pack your bags, grab your sense of adventure, and get ready to create unforgettable memories with your loved ones in the Heart of Dixie!

Gulf Shores Beach

(Southwest Alabama)

Gulf Shores Public Beach, Gulf Shores, AL 36542

(251) 968-1173 (Gulf Shores & Orange Beach Tourism)

Hours: Open 24/7

Admission: Free

Gulf Shores Beach is a fantastic destination for families with children of all ages. The wide, sandy beach and calm waters provide an ideal environment for various activities and attractions that cater to different age groups.

Activities and attractions for different age groups:

1. Toddlers and young children:
    - Building sandcastles and playing in the soft sand
    - Splashing in the shallow water and collecting seashells
    - Enjoying picnics and snacks in the shaded areas
    - Participating in family-friendly beach games like frisbee or beach ball toss
2. Older children and teenagers:
    - Swimming and boogie boarding in the gentle waves
    - Playing beach volleyball or soccer on the sand
    - Taking part in water sports like kayaking, paddleboarding, or surfing (rentals available nearby)
    - Exploring the nearby nature trails and wildlife at

Gulf State Park

3. Adults:
    ◦ Sunbathing and relaxing on the beach
    ◦ Fishing from the shore or nearby piers (fishing licenses required)
    ◦ Enjoying scenic walks along the beach or on the boardwalk
    ◦ Visiting local restaurants, bars, and shops in the Gulf Shores area

Amenities:

- Public restrooms and showers are available at multiple locations along the beach
- Picnic areas with tables and benches are provided for family gatherings
- Beach gear rentals (umbrellas, chairs, and beach toys) are available from nearby vendors
- Parking is available at public beach access points, some of which may require a fee during peak seasons

Handicap accessibility: Gulf Shores Beach is committed to providing accessibility for visitors with disabilities. The following amenities are available:

- Beach wheelchairs designed for use on sand are available for free rental at several locations along the beach
- Accessible restrooms and showers are provided at various beach access points
- Designated handicap parking spots are available at public beach access parking areas
- Ramps and boardwalks provide access to the beach from the parking areas

Stroller rentals: While there are no official stroller rentals directly on the beach, many nearby hotels, resorts, and vacation rental companies offer stroller rentals for guests. Visitors can also find stroller rentals at local baby equipment rental companies in the Gulf Shores area.

Other important information for visiting families:

- Be mindful of beach flag warnings that indicate surf conditions and potential hazards
- Apply sunscreen regularly and stay hydrated, especially during hot summer months
- Keep the beach clean by disposing of trash in the provided receptacles
- Be respectful of other beachgoers and wildlife by following beach rules and regulations
- In case of emergencies, contact the nearest lifeguard or call 911

Gulf Shores Beach offers a wide range of activities and amenities that cater to families with children of all ages. With its stunning natural beauty, well-maintained facilities, and commitment to accessibility, it is a perfect destination for a fun-filled family beach vacation.

Waterville USA

(Gulf Shores)

Address: 6601 Wahoo Lane, Gulf Shores, AL 36542

Phone: (251) 923-9200

Hours: Seasonal hours, typically open from late May to early September

Admission: General admission prices vary, but typically around $40 for adults and $30 for children (under 48 inches tall)

Waterville USA is an exciting destination for families with children of various ages. The park offers a wide range of water attractions, as well as additional activities that cater to different age groups.

Activities and attractions for different age groups:

1. Toddlers and young children:
    - Wa Wa World, a specially designed area for young children, features small slides, water sprays, and shallow pools
    - Waterville Hideaway, a play area with water slides, a dumping bucket, and water cannons
    - Dune Racer, a gentle slide that allows parents to ride along with their young children
2. Older children and teenagers:
    - Jet Stream, a thrilling water coaster that propels riders up and down steep slopes
    - Screaming Demon, a high-speed slide with sharp turns and sudden drops
    - Hurricane, a raft slide that sends riders swirling

through a large bowl before plunging into the pool below
- Lazy River, a relaxing float around the park on an inner tube
- Wave pool, a large pool with generated waves for swimming and playing

3. Adults:
- All water attractions are suitable for adults, with some slides having minimum height requirements
- Miniature golf course provides a fun activity for families to enjoy together
- Go-kart track offers an exciting racing experience for older children and adults
- Arcade with a variety of games and prizes for all ages

Amenities:

- Multiple dining options, including a pizza place, burger joint, and snack stands throughout the park
- Locker rentals are available to store personal belongings
- Cabanas can be rented for a more private and shaded area to relax
- Gift shops sell souvenirs, sunscreen, and other essentials
- Free parking is available on-site

Handicap accessibility: Waterville USA strives to provide an enjoyable experience for all guests, including those with disabilities. The following accommodations are available:

- Handicap parking is available near the entrance
- Most of the park's pathways are wheelchair accessible
- Some water attractions, such as the lazy river and wave

pool, are accessible for guests with limited mobility
- Assisted listening devices are available for hearing-impaired guests
- Service animals are welcome in the park

Stroller rentals: Stroller rentals are not available directly at Waterville USA. However, guests are welcome to bring their own strollers into the park. Strollers can be parked in designated areas near the attractions.

Other important information for visiting families:

- Height requirements apply for some water slides and attractions, so be sure to check before riding
- Life jackets are provided free of charge and are required for children under 48 inches tall
- Lockers and cabanas are available for rent on a first-come, first-served basis
- Outside food and beverages are not permitted inside the park, but picnic areas are available outside the main entrance
- Visitors should follow all posted safety rules and lifeguard instructions to ensure a safe and enjoyable experience

Waterville USA offers a fun-filled day for families with children of all ages. With its wide variety of water attractions, additional activities, and amenities designed for safety and convenience, it is a must-visit destination for families vacationing in the Gulf Shores area.

Alabama Gulf Coast
ZOO
and Safari Club Restaurant

Alabama Gulf Coast Zoo

(Gulf Shores)

Address: 20499 Oak Road East, Gulf Shores, AL 36542

Phone: (251) 968-5731

Hours: Daily from 9 AM to 4 PM (closed on major holidays)

Admission: Adults $15.95, Children (3-12) $11.95, Children under 3 free

The Alabama Gulf Coast Zoo is a wonderful destination for families with children of all ages. The zoo offers a variety of animal exhibits and interactive experiences that cater to different age groups.

Activities and attractions for different age groups:

1. Toddlers and young children:
    - Petting Zoo allows children to interact with friendly animals like goats, sheep, and rabbits
    - Reptile House features a variety of reptiles and amphibians, including turtles and snakes
    - Aviary offers a close-up view of colorful birds from around the world
    - Playground provides a fun space for children to run, climb, and play
2. Older children and teenagers:
    - Big cat exhibits showcase majestic lions, tigers, and other felines
    - Primate exhibits feature a variety of monkeys and lemurs
    - Bear exhibits allow visitors to observe black bears

and their natural behaviors
- Animal encounters and feedings provide opportunities to learn more about the animals and their care

3. Adults:
- All animal exhibits are engaging and educational for adults
- Keeper talks and animal demonstrations offer insights into animal behavior and conservation efforts
- Safari Club Restaurant provides a relaxing dining experience with a view of the zoo grounds

Amenities:

- Safari Cafe offers a variety of food and beverage options, including burgers, pizzas, and ice cream
- Gift shop sells souvenirs, toys, and animal-related merchandise
- Picnic areas are available for families who wish to bring their own food and enjoy a meal on the zoo grounds
- Stroller and wheelchair rentals are available at the zoo entrance
- Free parking is available on-site

Handicap accessibility: The Alabama Gulf Coast Zoo is committed to providing an accessible experience for all visitors. The following accommodations are available:

- Handicap parking is available near the entrance
- The zoo grounds are wheelchair accessible, with paved pathways throughout
- Wheelchair rentals are available at the zoo entrance

- Service animals are welcome in the zoo

Stroller rentals: Single and double strollers are available for rent at the zoo entrance on a first-come, first-served basis. Stroller rental fees are affordable, and rentals can be made for the entire day.

Other important information for visiting families:

- The zoo is open rain or shine, but some exhibits may close during inclement weather
- Visitors should wear comfortable walking shoes and bring sunscreen, hats, and water, especially during the summer months
- Some animal encounters and feedings require an additional fee and have limited availability, so it's best to check the schedule and make reservations in advance
- The zoo hosts special events throughout the year, such as "Boo at the Zoo" during Halloween and "Zoo Lights" during the holiday season

The Alabama Gulf Coast Zoo provides a fun and educational experience for families with children of all ages. With its diverse animal exhibits, interactive experiences, and welcoming amenities, it is a must-visit attraction for families vacationing in the Gulf Shores area.

Fairhope Pier

(Southwest Alabama)

Address: 1 Beach Road, Fairhope, AL 36532

Phone: (251) 928-1148 (Fairhope Welcome Center)

Hours: Open 24/7

Admission: Free

The Fairhope Pier is a beautiful and historic attraction that offers a variety of activities for families with children of different ages. The pier and surrounding area provide a scenic and relaxing environment for visitors to enjoy.

Activities and attractions for different age groups:

1. Toddlers and young children:
    - Strolling along the pier and enjoying the fresh air and scenic views
    - Watching boats and marine life from the pier
    - Playing in the adjacent park area, which features a playground and open spaces for running and playing
    - Enjoying a picnic or snack in the park or on the pier benches
2. Older children and teenagers:
    - Fishing from the pier (fishing equipment can be rented nearby)
    - Participating in outdoor activities like kite flying or frisbee in the park area
    - Exploring the nearby downtown Fairhope area,

which features shops, restaurants, and an ice cream parlor
- Attending festivals and events held on the pier throughout the year

3. Adults:
- Enjoying scenic walks along the pier and taking in the beautiful views of Mobile Bay
- Fishing from the pier or nearby areas (fishing licenses required)
- Relaxing on benches and watching the sunset or sunrise over the water
- Visiting local shops, galleries, and restaurants in the charming downtown Fairhope area
- Attending concerts, art shows, and other events held on the pier

Amenities:

- Benches are located along the pier for visitors to sit and relax
- Trash receptacles are available to help keep the area clean
- Public restrooms are located in the adjacent park area
- Free parking is available near the pier and in the surrounding downtown area
- Fishing equipment rentals are available at nearby shops

Handicap accessibility: The Fairhope Pier and surrounding area are accessible for visitors with disabilities. The following accommodations are available:

- The pier is wheelchair accessible, with a flat, even surface
- Handicap parking is available in the nearby parking areas
- Public restrooms in the adjacent park area are ADA-

compliant

Stroller accessibility: The pier is stroller-friendly, with a flat, even surface that is easy to navigate. Families with strollers can easily access the pier and enjoy a leisurely walk along the water.

Other important information for visiting families:

- The pier is open 24/7, allowing visitors to enjoy the area at any time of day
- Fishing from the pier does not require a license, but fishing in other areas may require a valid Alabama fishing license
- The pier and surrounding area can be breezy, so visitors should bring jackets or sweaters, especially during cooler months
- Sun protection, such as hats and sunscreen, is recommended for daytime visits
- Visitors should be mindful of posted rules and regulations, such as not climbing on the pier railings or leaving trash behind

The Fairhope Pier is a delightful destination that offers a perfect blend of relaxation, scenic beauty, and outdoor activities for families with children of all ages. With its rich history, stunning views, and convenient amenities, the pier is a must-visit attraction for those exploring the charming coastal town of Fairhope, Alabama.

Bellingrath Gardens and Home

(Theodore)

Address: 12401 Bellingrath Gardens Road, Theodore, AL 36582

Phone: (251) 973-2217

Hours: Daily from 8 AM to 5 PM (closed on major holidays)

Admission: Adults $27.54, Children (5-12) $14.95, Children under 5 free

Bellingrath Gardens and Home is a beautiful and historic estate that offers a variety of activities and attractions for families with children of different ages. The gardens and home provide a stunning and educational environment for visitors to explore.

Activities and attractions for different age groups:

1. Toddlers and young children:
    - Exploring the colorful and fragrant flowers in the gardens
    - Enjoying the serene atmosphere and beauty of nature
    - Participating in scavenger hunts or garden-themed activities provided by the estate
    - Picnicking on the beautiful grounds
2. Older children and teenagers:
    - Learning about the history and architecture of the Bellingrath Home during guided tours
    - Discovering the diverse plant life and ecosystems in the gardens
    - Participating in educational programs and

workshops offered by the estate
  - Enjoying outdoor activities like birdwatching or photography

3. Adults:
  - Admiring the stunning beauty and design of the formal gardens
  - Touring the historic Bellingrath Home and learning about its antiques and artifacts
  - Attending special events, such as the Magic Christmas in Lights or the Fall Outdoor Cascading Chrysanthemums display
  - Relaxing and unwinding in the peaceful atmosphere of the gardens
  - Participating in guided tours or workshops focused on gardening, history, or art

Amenities:

- Bellingrath Gift Shop offers a variety of souvenirs, plants, and garden-related items
- Magnolia Café serves lunch daily and offers a selection of sandwiches, salads, and desserts
- Picnic tables are available throughout the gardens for visitors who wish to bring their own food
- Restrooms and drinking fountains are located throughout the estate
- Ample parking is available on-site

Handicap accessibility: Bellingrath Gardens and Home is committed to providing an accessible experience for all visitors. The following accommodations are available:

- Handicap parking is available near the entrance

- The gardens feature paved pathways that are wheelchair accessible
- The first floor of the Bellingrath Home is wheelchair accessible
- Wheelchair rentals are available at the gift shop
- Service animals are welcome in the gardens and home

Stroller accessibility: The gardens feature paved pathways that are stroller-friendly, making it easy for families with young children to explore the estate. Strollers can be rented at the gift shop on a first-come, first-served basis.

Other important information for visiting families:

- The estate is open daily, but hours may vary by season, so it's best to check the website or call ahead
- Guided tours of the Bellingrath Home are offered throughout the day, with tickets available for purchase at the admissions building
- The Magic Christmas in Lights event is a popular attraction during the holiday season, featuring over 1,100 set pieces and 3 million lights
- The estate offers a variety of educational programs and workshops for visitors of all ages, including school field trips and summer camps
- Visitors should wear comfortable walking shoes and bring sunscreen, hats, and water, especially during the summer months

Bellingrath Gardens and Home is a must-visit destination for families with children of all ages. With its stunning gardens, historic home, and engaging educational programs, the estate offers a unique and enriching experience that combines natural beauty, history, and learning. Whether exploring the colorful gardens or discovering the antiques and artifacts in the Bellingrath Home, families will create lasting memories at this beautiful and serene attraction.

Huntsville Botanical Garden

(Northwest Alabama)

Address: 4747 Bob Wallace Ave SW, Huntsville, AL 35805

Phone: (256) 830-4447

Hours: Tuesday-Saturday 9 AM - 5 PM, Sunday 11 AM - 5 PM (Closed Mondays)

Admission: Adults $18, Children (3-18) $12, Children under 3 free

The Huntsville Botanical Garden is a wonderful destination for families with children of all ages. The garden offers a variety of themed areas, activities, and attractions that cater to different age groups and interests.

Activities and attractions for different age groups:

1. Toddlers and young children:
   - Children's Garden features interactive play areas, including a splash pad, a dinosaur dig, and a rainbow garden
   - Little Sprouts Garden offers hands-on gardening experiences for young children
   - Stroller-friendly paths throughout the garden allow for easy exploration
   - Children's story time and crafts are offered regularly
2. Older children and teenagers:
   - Butterfly House allows visitors to observe and learn about various butterfly species
   - Lewis Birding Trail offers opportunities for

- birdwatching and nature photography
  - Huntsville Botanical Garden features a variety of themed gardens, such as the Herb Garden and the Daylily Garden, which provide educational experiences
  - Seasonal events like the Scarecrow Trail and the Galaxy of Lights offer fun and engaging activities

3. Adults:
   - Exploring the diverse themed gardens, such as the Purdy Butterfly House, the Aquatic Garden, and the Japanese Garden
   - Attending gardening workshops, lectures, and classes offered throughout the year
   - Enjoying seasonal events like the Spring Plant Sale and the Galaxy of Lights
   - Relaxing and unwinding in the peaceful atmosphere of the gardens
   - Participating in guided tours or volunteering opportunities

Amenities:

- The Garden Gift Shop offers a variety of souvenirs, plants, and gardening-related items
- The Dogwood Café serves light lunches, snacks, and beverages
- Picnic tables and benches are located throughout the garden for visitors to relax and enjoy their own food
- Restrooms and drinking fountains are available in various locations
- Free parking is available on-site

Handicap accessibility: The Huntsville Botanical Garden is committed to providing an accessible experience for all visitors. The following accommodations are available:

- Handicap parking is available near the entrance
- The majority of the garden's paths are wheelchair accessible
- Wheelchairs are available for rent at the admission desk
- The Butterfly House and restrooms are wheelchair accessible
- Service animals are welcome in the garden

Stroller accessibility: The garden features paved paths that are stroller-friendly, making it easy for families with young children to explore the various areas. Strollers can be rented at the admission desk on a first-come, first-served basis.

Other important information for visiting families:

- The garden is open year-round, but hours may vary by season, so it's best to check the website or call ahead
- Seasonal events and activities may require separate tickets or reservations, so it's important to plan ahead
- The Garden Gift Shop and Dogwood Café are open during garden hours
- The garden offers a variety of educational programs, summer camps, and field trip opportunities for children and families
- Visitors should wear comfortable walking shoes and bring sunscreen, hats, and water, especially during the summer months

The Huntsville Botanical Garden is a must-visit destination for families looking to connect with nature, learn about plants and wildlife, and enjoy a peaceful and beautiful setting. With its diverse themed gardens, engaging educational programs, and family-friendly amenities, the garden offers a unique and enriching experience for visitors of all ages. Whether exploring the Children's Garden, observing butterflies in the Purdy Butterfly House, or simply relaxing amidst the stunning natural beauty, families will create lasting memories at this premier botanical garden in Northwest Alabama.

U.S. Space &
Rocket Center

U.S. Space and Rocket Center

(Huntsville)

Address: 1 Tranquility Base, Huntsville, AL 35805

Phone: (800) 637-7223

Hours: Daily from 9 AM to 5 PM (Closed on major holidays)

Admission: Adults $25, Children (5-12) $17, Children under 5 free

The U.S. Space and Rocket Center is an exciting and educational destination that offers a wide range of activities and attractions for families with children of all ages. The center provides an immersive experience that sparks curiosity and encourages learning about space exploration and science.

Activities and attractions for different age groups:

1. Toddlers and young children:
    - Kids Cosmos play area features interactive exhibits and play structures designed for younger children
    - Spark!Lab encourages hands-on learning and exploration of science and technology concepts
    - Rocket Park offers an up-close look at real rockets and spacecraft, which can be exciting for young children
    - The Mars Climbing Wall allows children to experience a simulated Martian terrain
2. Older children and teenagers:
    - Space Camp programs offer age-appropriate, immersive experiences that allow participants to

train like astronauts and learn about space exploration
- ◦ Simulators, such as the Space Shot and G-Force Accelerator, provide thrilling experiences that mimic the sensations of space travel
- ◦ Interactive exhibits, like the ISS: Science on Orbit and Explorer 1 Discovery, engage visitors in learning about the history and science of space exploration
- ◦ The National Geographic Theater presents educational films on a variety of science and space-related topics

3. Adults:
- ◦ Guided tours offer in-depth insights into the history and science of space exploration
- ◦ Saturn V Hall showcases a full-scale replica of the Saturn V rocket, along with other historic artifacts and exhibits
- ◦ Planetarium shows provide a fascinating look at the cosmos and the latest astronomical discoveries
- ◦ The U.S. Space and Rocket Center hosts special events, lectures, and workshops throughout the year, catering to a wide range of interests

Amenities:

- The Mars Grill and Rocket Fuel food court offer a variety of dining options
- The Space Shop sells space-related souvenirs, books, and gifts
- Strollers and wheelchairs are available for rent at the Guest Services desk
- Lockers are available for rent to store personal belongings

- Free parking is available on-site

Handicap accessibility: The U.S. Space and Rocket Center is committed to providing an accessible experience for all visitors. The following accommodations are available:

- Handicap parking is available near the entrance
- The majority of the center's exhibits and attractions are wheelchair accessible
- Wheelchairs are available for rent at the Guest Services desk
- Assistive listening devices are available for the National Geographic Theater and the Spacedome IMAX Theater
- Service animals are welcome in the center

Stroller accessibility: The center is stroller-friendly, with wide, smooth paths that are easy to navigate. Strollers can be rented at the Guest Services desk on a first-come, first-served basis.

Other important information for visiting families:

- The center is open year-round, but hours may vary during peak seasons and holidays, so it's best to check the website or call ahead
- Some attractions, such as the Space Shot and G-Force Accelerator, have height and weight restrictions
- Space Camp programs require advance registration and have specific age requirements
- The center offers a variety of educational programs, field trip opportunities, and homeschool days throughout the year
- Visitors should wear comfortable walking shoes and be prepared to spend several hours exploring the exhibits and

attractions

The U.S. Space and Rocket Center is a must-visit destination for families who are interested in space exploration, science, and technology. With its engaging exhibits, interactive experiences, and educational programs, the center offers a unique and inspiring experience that encourages learning and sparks the imagination. Whether exploring the Rocket Park, attending Space Camp, or watching a stunning film in the Spacedome IMAX Theater, families will create unforgettable memories at this world-class attraction in Huntsville, Alabama.

Harmony Park Safari

(Huntsville)

Address: 431 Murphy Hill Rd, Huntsville, AL 35811

Phone: (256) 423-6800

Hours: Daily from 9 AM to 5 PM (Closed on major holidays)

Admission: Adults $18.95, Children (3-12) $11.95, Children under 3 free

Harmony Park Safari is a fantastic destination for families with children of all ages who love animals and enjoy unique outdoor experiences. The park offers a chance to observe and interact with a variety of exotic animals in a natural setting, providing both entertainment and educational opportunities.

Activities and attractions for different age groups:

1. Toddlers and young children:
     - Observing animals from the safety of the family vehicle during the drive-through safari
     - Feeding animals like zebras and camels from the car with provided food pellets
     - Petting and interacting with smaller, friendly animals in the walk-through area
     - Enjoying the park's playground equipment and picnic areas
2. Older children and teenagers:
     - Learning about the animals and their habitats through educational talks and animal encounters
     - Taking photos and videos of the exotic animals in

        their natural-like environments
- Participating in guided tours and special events, such as behind-the-scenes experiences or holiday-themed activities
- Exploring the gift shop and learning about animal conservation efforts

3. Adults:
   - Appreciating the unique opportunity to observe exotic animals up close in a safari-like setting
   - Participating in educational talks and animal encounters to gain a deeper understanding of the animals and their care
   - Enjoying the scenic drive through the park and the natural beauty of the surroundings
   - Relaxing in the picnic areas and soaking in the peaceful atmosphere

Amenities:

- The Safari Cafe offers a variety of snacks, drinks, and light meals
- The gift shop sells animal-related souvenirs, toys, and educational materials
- Picnic tables and benches are available throughout the park for visitors to relax and enjoy their own food
- Restrooms are located at the entrance and exit of the park
- Free parking is available on-site

Handicap accessibility: Harmony Park Safari strives to provide an accessible experience for visitors with disabilities. The following accommodations are available:

- The drive-through safari is accessible for visitors with

mobility issues, as they can remain in their vehicles
- The walk-through area has mostly flat, gravel paths that may be navigable for some wheelchairs and strollers
- Service animals are permitted in the park, but not in the walk-through area due to the presence of other animals

Stroller accessibility: Families with strollers can easily enjoy the drive-through safari portion of the park. However, the walk-through area may have some uneven or gravel paths that could be challenging for some strollers. It's recommended to use a stroller with larger, sturdy wheels or to carry smaller children when necessary.

Other important information for visiting families:

- The park is open year-round, but hours may vary during the winter months, so it's best to check the website or call ahead
- Visitors must remain in their vehicles during the drive-through safari and follow all posted safety guidelines
- Food pellets for feeding the animals are available for purchase at the entrance and should be the only food given to the animals
- Some animal encounters and guided tours may require advance reservations and additional fees
- Visitors should dress for the weather and wear comfortable, closed-toe shoes for walking in the walk-through area

Harmony Park Safari offers a memorable and educational experience for families who want to observe and interact with exotic animals in a unique setting. With its combination of drive-through and walk-through areas, the park provides a safe and engaging way for children and adults to learn about and appreciate these fascinating creatures. By following the park's guidelines and taking advantage of the educational opportunities, families can make the most of their visit to this one-of-a-kind attraction in Huntsville, Alabama.

Dismals Canyon

(Phil Campbell)

Address: 631 Dismals Canyon Rd, Phil Campbell, AL 35581

Phone: (256) 757-5916

Hours: Daily from 8 AM to sunset (Closed on major holidays)

Admission: Adults $10, Children (6-12) $5, Children under 6 free

Dismals Canyon is a stunning natural attraction that offers families with children of all ages a chance to explore, learn, and enjoy the great outdoors. With its unique geological features, diverse wildlife, and range of activities, the canyon provides an unforgettable experience for nature enthusiasts and adventurers alike.

Activities and attractions for different age groups:

1. Toddlers and young children:
   - Enjoying short, easy hikes on the canyon's well-maintained trails under close adult supervision
   - Exploring the shallow, gentle streams and splashing in the water
   - Observing the diverse plant life and wildlife, such as birds and butterflies
   - Participating in nature-themed scavenger hunts or guided activities designed for young children
2. Older children and teenagers:
   - Hiking the more challenging trails and discovering hidden waterfalls and unique rock formations
   - Learning about the canyon's geology, history, and

ecology through educational programs and guided tours
  ◦ Fishing in the designated areas of the canyon's streams (with proper licenses and adult supervision)
  ◦ Participating in outdoor skills workshops, such as rock climbing or wilderness survival
3. Adults:
  ◦ Embarking on scenic hikes and enjoying the tranquil beauty of the canyon
  ◦ Photographing the stunning landscapes, waterfalls, and wildlife
  ◦ Attending guided night tours to witness the unique bioluminescent insects (Dismalites) that inhabit the canyon
  ◦ Enjoying a peaceful picnic in the designated areas or simply relaxing amidst nature
  ◦ Camping overnight to fully immerse in the canyon's serene environment

Amenities:

- The country store at the entrance offers snacks, drinks, and basic camping supplies
- Picnic tables and grills are available in designated areas throughout the canyon
- Restrooms and changing rooms are located near the canyon's entrance
- Free parking is available on-site

Handicap accessibility: Due to the rugged nature of the canyon, many of the trails and attractions may not be fully accessible for individuals with mobility issues. However, some accommodations are available:

- The boardwalk trail near the entrance is relatively flat and may be navigable for some wheelchairs and strollers
- Visitors with mobility issues can still enjoy the scenic views from the canyon's rim and picnic areas
- Service animals are permitted on the trails and in the canyon

Stroller accessibility: The rugged terrain and narrow trails may make it challenging to navigate with strollers. It's recommended to use a sturdy, all-terrain stroller or to carry younger children in a child carrier when hiking the trails. The boardwalk trail near the entrance is the most stroller-friendly option.

Other important information for visiting families:

- The canyon is open year-round, but some trails and areas may be closed during inclement weather or for maintenance, so it's best to check the website or call ahead
- Visitors should wear sturdy, closed-toe shoes and bring plenty of water and snacks for their hikes
- Insect repellent and sun protection are recommended, especially during the warmer months
- Swimming is not permitted in the canyon's streams, but visitors can wade and splash in designated areas
- Visitors should follow all posted safety guidelines and stay on marked trails to protect the delicate ecosystem and ensure their own safety

Dismals Canyon is a must-visit destination for families who love nature, adventure, and learning. With its awe-inspiring beauty, diverse wildlife, and range of outdoor activities, the canyon offers a unique and enriching experience for visitors of all ages. By following the park's guidelines and taking advantage of the educational opportunities, families can create lasting memories while exploring this natural wonder in Phil Campbell, Alabama.

Unclaimed
Baggage

Unclaimed Baggage Center

(Scottsboro)

Address: 510 West Willow St, Scottsboro, AL 35768

Phone: (256) 259-1525

Hours: Monday-Friday 9 AM - 6 PM, Saturday 8 AM - 6 PM, Sunday 10 AM - 6 PM

Admission: Free

The Unclaimed Baggage Center is a one-of-a-kind attraction that offers families a unique shopping and learning experience. While the center may not have traditional family-oriented activities, it provides an opportunity for children to explore, discover, and learn about the fascinating world of lost and found.

Activities and attractions for different age groups:

1. Toddlers and young children:
    - Exploring the colorful and diverse array of merchandise with their parents
    - Discovering unique toys, stuffed animals, and children's clothing
    - Learning about the concept of lost and found items
2. Older children and teenagers:
    - Searching for unique and trendy clothing, accessories, and gadgets
    - Exploring the museum section to learn about the history and unusual items found in unclaimed baggage

- Developing an understanding of responsible consumerism and the importance of keeping track of personal belongings
- Participating in a scavenger hunt to find specific items throughout the store

3. Adults:
    - Browsing the vast selection of merchandise for great deals on clothing, electronics, and other items
    - Discovering rare and unusual finds, such as historical artifacts or celebrity memorabilia
    - Learning about the process of how unclaimed baggage is acquired and sold
    - Enjoying the thrill of the treasure hunt and the potential for unexpected discoveries

Amenities:

- The center has a café offering snacks, drinks, and light meals
- Restrooms are available for customers
- Free parking is available in the center's parking lot

Handicap accessibility: The Unclaimed Baggage Center is committed to providing an accessible shopping experience for all visitors. The following accommodations are available:

- The store has wide aisles and is wheelchair accessible
- Handicap parking spaces are available near the entrance
- Service animals are permitted in the store

Stroller accessibility: The store's wide aisles and spacious layout make it easy to navigate with strollers. However, during busy periods, it may be more challenging to maneuver through the crowds with a stroller.

Other important information for visiting families:

- The center is open year-round, but hours may vary during holidays, so it's best to check the website or call ahead
- The inventory at the Unclaimed Baggage Center is constantly changing, so each visit offers a new experience
- Some items, such as electronics and jewelry, may be priced higher than others due to their value or rarity
- The center occasionally hosts special events and sales, which can be found on their website or social media pages

The Unclaimed Baggage Center offers a unique and engaging experience for families, combining the excitement of shopping with the opportunity to learn about the fascinating world of lost and found. While it may not have traditional family-oriented activities, the center provides a chance for children to explore, discover, and develop an appreciation for responsible consumerism. With its wide array of merchandise and ever-changing inventory, the Unclaimed Baggage Center is sure to provide a memorable experience for visitors of all ages in Scottsboro, Alabama.

Gulf State Park

(Gulf Shores)

Address: 20115 State Park Rd, Gulf Shores, AL 36542

Phone: (251) 948-7275

Hours: Open daily from 7 AM to Sunset

Admission: $6 per vehicle

Gulf State Park is a fantastic destination for families looking to enjoy a variety of outdoor activities and appreciate the natural beauty of the Alabama Gulf Coast. The park offers something for every age group, making it an ideal spot for a family vacation or a day trip.

Activities and attractions for different age groups:

1. Toddlers and young children:
    - Playing in the soft sand and shallow water along the beach
    - Building sandcastles and collecting seashells
    - Exploring the nature center and participating in age-appropriate educational programs
    - Enjoying picnics in the designated areas and playgrounds
2. Older children and teenagers:
    - Swimming, boogie boarding, and surfing in the Gulf waters
    - Fishing from the pier or along the beach (with proper licenses)
    - Hiking and biking on the park's extensive trail network

- Participating in ranger-led programs and nature walks
- Renting kayaks or paddleboards to explore the park's lakes and waterways

3. Adults:
   - Relaxing on the beach and soaking up the sun
   - Enjoying scenic walks or bike rides along the trails and boardwalks
   - Birdwatching and wildlife observation in the park's diverse habitats
   - Fishing from the pier or beach (with proper licenses)
   - Camping in the park's modern or primitive campsites

Amenities:

- The park has several beach pavilions with restrooms, showers, and picnic tables
- Beach equipment rentals, including umbrellas, chairs, and kayaks, are available
- The camp store offers snacks, drinks, and basic camping supplies
- Laundry facilities and a dump station are available for campers
- Playgrounds and picnic areas are located throughout the park

Handicap accessibility: Gulf State Park strives to provide an accessible outdoor experience for visitors with disabilities. The following accommodations are available:

- Beach wheelchairs are available for free rental at the beach

pavilions
- Many of the park's trails and boardwalks are wheelchair accessible
- Accessible restrooms and showers are located at the beach pavilions and campgrounds
- Some campsites are designed to be accessible for visitors with disabilities

Stroller accessibility: The park's boardwalks and some trails are stroller-friendly, allowing families with young children to easily explore the natural surroundings. However, some of the more rugged hiking trails may not be suitable for strollers.

Other important information for visiting families:

- The park is open year-round, but some facilities and services may have limited hours during the off-season
- Visitors should be aware of beach flag warnings indicating surf conditions and potential hazards
- Insect repellent and sun protection are recommended, especially during the warmer months
- Pets are allowed in designated areas of the park but must be kept on a leash
- Alcoholic beverages are prohibited in the park

Gulf State Park is a must-visit destination for families looking to enjoy the great outdoors and experience the natural beauty of the Alabama Gulf Coast. With its wide range of activities, amenities, and accessibility features, the park offers something for every age group and interest. Whether camping, hiking, fishing, or simply relaxing on the beach, families will create lasting memories at this stunning state park in Gulf Shores, Alabama.

OWA

(Foley)

Address: 151 OWA Blvd, Foley, AL 36535

Phone: (251) 923-2111

Hours: Varies by season and attraction

Admission: Prices vary for different attractions and packages

OWA is a fantastic entertainment destination that offers a wide range of activities and attractions for families with children of all ages. With its combination of thrilling rides, shopping, dining, and other entertainment options, OWA provides an exciting and memorable experience for the whole family.

Activities and attractions for different age groups:

1. Toddlers and young children:
    - Enjoying gentler rides like the Honey Pot Bear Spin and the Flying Carousel
    - Exploring the outdoor playground and splash pad area
    - Participating in kid-friendly shows and character meet-and-greets
    - Playing mini-golf at the Glow-in-the-Dark Mini Golf course
2. Older children and teenagers:
    - Experiencing thrilling rides like the Rollin' Thunder roller coaster and the Freedom Flyer spinning ride
    - Playing arcade games and winning prizes at the

Midway Games area
- Challenging friends and family at the bowling alley or laser tag arena
- Watching a movie at the state-of-the-art cinema

3. Adults:
- Shopping at the variety of retail stores and specialty shops
- Enjoying a meal or drink at one of the many dining options, from quick bites to sit-down restaurants
- Relaxing at the Island Amphitheater while enjoying live music or performances
- Participating in seasonal events and festivals held at OWA throughout the year

Amenities:

- Multiple dining options, ranging from quick-service restaurants to sit-down dining
- Restrooms and changing facilities located throughout the park
- Stroller and wheelchair rentals available
- Free parking in the on-site parking lot
- Lockers available for rent to store personal belongings

Handicap accessibility:

OWA strives to provide an accessible and enjoyable experience for all guests. The following accommodations are available:

- Wheelchair-accessible routes throughout the park
- Accessible restrooms and seating areas
- Some rides and attractions are designed to accommodate

guests with disabilities

- Service animals are welcome in the park

Stroller accessibility:

OWA is stroller-friendly, with wide, paved walkways throughout the park. Stroller rentals are also available for families who prefer not to bring their own.

Other important information for visiting families:

- Operating hours vary by season and attraction, so it's best to check the official website or call ahead for the most up-to-date information
- Some rides and attractions have height and weight restrictions for safety purposes
- Guests can purchase individual ride tickets, day passes, or season passes, depending on their preferences and the length of their visit
- Special events and festivals are held throughout the year, offering additional entertainment and activities for families

OWA is a must-visit destination for families looking for a fun-filled day or a memorable vacation experience. With its diverse range of attractions and amenities, OWA caters to the interests and needs of all age groups, ensuring that everyone in the family has a great time. Whether you're seeking thrills, shopping, dining, or entertainment, OWA has something to offer, making it a top choice for families visiting Foley, Alabama.

Tanger Outlets

(Foley)

Address: 2601 Bass Pro Dr, Foley, AL 36535

Phone: (251) 943-9300

Hours: Monday-Saturday 10 AM - 9 PM, Sunday 10 AM - 7 PM

Admission: Free

Tanger Outlets in Foley is a fantastic destination for families looking to enjoy a day of shopping, dining, and entertainment. While primarily a shopping center, Tanger Outlets offers a variety of activities and amenities that cater to families with children of all ages.

Activities and attractions for different age groups:

1. Toddlers and young children:
    - Playing in the designated children's play areas, which feature soft play structures and interactive elements
    - Enjoying the outdoor green spaces and seating areas with their families
    - Participating in kid-friendly events and activities organized by the mall, such as face painting or storytelling
2. Older children and teenagers:
    - Shopping for clothing, accessories, and toys at their favorite brand-name stores
    - Grabbing a bite to eat at one of the many dining options, from fast food to sit-down restaurants

- ○ Enjoying live music performances or seasonal festivals held at the mall
- ○ Participating in scavenger hunts or other challenges organized by the mall or individual stores

3. Adults:
- ○ Taking advantage of deep discounts and special promotions at over 120 brand-name outlet stores
- ○ Enjoying a leisurely shopping experience in the pleasant outdoor environment
- ○ Relaxing in the ample seating areas or outdoor green spaces
- ○ Attending special events, such as food festivals or holiday celebrations

Amenities:

- Several dining options, ranging from quick bites to sit-down restaurants
- Restrooms and changing facilities located throughout the mall
- Ample seating areas and outdoor green spaces for relaxation
- Free parking in the on-site parking lot
- Free Wi-Fi throughout the mall

Handicap accessibility: Tanger Outlets Foley is committed to providing an accessible shopping experience for all visitors. The following accommodations are available:

- Wide, level walkways throughout the mall, suitable for wheelchairs and strollers
- Accessible restrooms and seating areas

- Designated handicap parking spaces close to the mall entrances
- Service animals are welcome in the mall

Stroller accessibility: Tanger Outlets Foley is stroller-friendly, with wide, level walkways throughout the mall. Families can easily navigate the mall with their strollers, making it convenient to shop with young children.

Other important information for visiting families:

- Operating hours may vary during holidays or special events, so it's best to check the official website or call ahead for the most up-to-date information
- Some stores may have their own promotions, discounts, or loyalty programs, so it's worth checking with individual retailers
- The mall hosts various events and activities throughout the year, such as live music, seasonal festivals, and holiday celebrations, which can add to the overall family experience
- Strollers, wheelchairs, and other mobility aids are permitted in the mall, making it easily accessible for families with diverse needs

Tanger Outlets Foley offers a fantastic combination of shopping, dining, and entertainment for families, all within a pleasant and accessible outdoor environment. With a wide range of brand-name stores, deep discounts, and family-friendly amenities, Tanger Outlets provides an enjoyable day out for family members of all ages. Whether you're looking for a full day of shopping or just a few hours of browsing, Tanger Outlets Foley is a great destination for families in the Foley, Alabama area.

Dauphin Island Sea Lab

(Dauphin Island)

Address: 101 Bienville Blvd, Dauphin Island, AL 36528

Phone: (251) 861-2141

Hours: Wednesday-Sunday 10 AM - 6 PM (Closed Monday and Tuesday) Admission: Adults $6, Children (5-18) $4, Children under 5 free

The Dauphin Island Sea Lab is an excellent destination for families looking to combine education and entertainment while exploring the wonders of marine life and coastal ecosystems. With its interactive exhibits, aquariums, and hands-on activities, the Sea Lab offers engaging experiences for children of all ages.

Activities and attractions for different age groups:

1. Toddlers and young children:
    - Observing colorful fish and other marine life in the aquariums
    - Touching live marine animals in the touch tanks under staff supervision
    - Participating in age-appropriate, hands-on activities and crafts related to marine life
    - Enjoying the "Just for Kids" exhibit area designed specifically for younger children
2. Older children and teenagers:
    - Exploring the interactive exhibits to learn about marine ecosystems, conservation, and research
    - Participating in educational programs, such as the "Discover Dauphin Island" or "Coastal Explorers"

  programs
  - Engaging in hands-on activities, like microscope investigations or dissections (in certain programs)
  - Joining guided tours to learn more about the Sea Lab's research projects and marine life

3. Adults:
  - Learning about the diverse marine life and coastal ecosystems of the Gulf of Mexico
  - Participating in guided tours and educational programs to gain a deeper understanding of marine conservation and research
  - Observing the Sea Lab's ongoing research projects and efforts to protect marine habitats
  - Enjoying the stunning views of Dauphin Island and the Gulf of Mexico from the Sea Lab's location

Amenities:

- The Sea Lab Gift Shop offers a variety of marine-themed souvenirs, books, and educational toys
- Restrooms and changing facilities are available on-site
- Picnic tables and benches are located outside the Sea Lab for visitors to enjoy their own snacks or meals
- Free parking is available in the Sea Lab's parking lot

Handicap accessibility: The Dauphin Island Sea Lab is committed to providing an accessible experience for all visitors. The following accommodations are available:

- The Sea Lab's main exhibit area is wheelchair accessible
- Handicap parking spaces are available in the parking lot
- Service animals are welcome in the Sea Lab

Stroller accessibility: The Sea Lab's main exhibit area is stroller-friendly, with wide, level pathways that are easy to navigate. Families with strollers can comfortably explore the exhibits and aquariums.

Other important information for visiting families:

- The Sea Lab is open Wednesday through Sunday, so it's important to plan your visit accordingly
- Some educational programs and guided tours may require advance registration and additional fees
- The Sea Lab may have special events or temporary exhibits throughout the year, so it's worth checking their website or calling ahead for the most up-to-date information
- Visitors are encouraged to respect the marine life and follow the guidance of Sea Lab staff to ensure a safe and enjoyable experience for all

The Dauphin Island Sea Lab provides a unique and enriching experience for families, combining education and entertainment in a beautiful coastal setting. With its focus on marine life, conservation, and research, the Sea Lab offers valuable lessons and unforgettable memories for visitors of all ages. Whether exploring the interactive exhibits, participating in hands-on activities, or joining guided tours, families will leave the Dauphin Island Sea Lab with a deeper appreciation for the wonders of the ocean and the importance of protecting marine habitats.

Dothan National Botanical Garden

(Dothan)

Address: 5002 W Main St, Dothan, AL 36305

Phone: (334) 793-3700

Hours: Tuesday-Saturday 9 AM - 5 PM, Sunday 12 PM - 5 PM (Closed Mondays)

Admission: Adults $5, Children (3-12) $3, Children under 3 free

The Dothan National Botanical Garden is a fantastic destination for families looking to spend a day outdoors, enjoying nature and learning about plants, wildlife, and conservation. With its diverse themed gardens and engaging educational programs, the botanical garden offers a fun and enriching experience for children of all ages.

Activities and attractions for different age groups:

1. Toddlers and young children:
    - Exploring the Children's Discovery Garden, which features interactive play elements and sensory experiences
    - Observing butterflies and other pollinators in the Butterfly Garden
    - Participating in age-appropriate, hands-on activities and crafts related to plants and nature
    - Enjoying the playground and picnic areas with their families
2. Older children and teenagers:
    - Learning about different plant species and their adaptations in the themed gardens

- Participating in educational programs, such as guided tours, workshops, or scavenger hunts
- Discovering the importance of environmental conservation and sustainability
- Exploring the nature center exhibits to learn about local flora and fauna

3. Adults:
   - Admiring the beauty and serenity of the various themed gardens
   - Learning about gardening techniques, plant care, and landscape design through workshops or guided tours
   - Enjoying a leisurely walk or picnic in the peaceful surroundings
   - Visiting the gift shop to purchase plants, gardening supplies, or nature-themed souvenirs

Amenities:

- The gift shop offers a variety of plants, gardening supplies, books, and nature-themed souvenirs
- Restrooms and drinking fountains are available throughout the garden
- Picnic tables and benches are located in designated areas for visitors to enjoy their own snacks or meals
- Free parking is available in the botanical garden's parking lot

Handicap accessibility: The Dothan National Botanical Garden strives to provide an accessible experience for all visitors. The following accommodations are available:

- Many of the garden paths are wheelchair accessible, with

some paved or compacted gravel surfaces

- Handicap parking spaces are available in the parking lot
- Service animals are welcome in the botanical garden

Stroller accessibility: The botanical garden's paths are generally stroller-friendly, with some paved or compacted gravel surfaces. However, some areas may have uneven terrain or narrow passages, so families with strollers should be prepared to navigate these areas carefully.

Other important information for visiting families:

- The botanical garden is closed on Mondays, so it's important to plan your visit accordingly
- Some educational programs and workshops may require advance registration and additional fees
- The garden may have special events or seasonal displays throughout the year, so it's worth checking their website or calling ahead for the most up-to-date information
- Visitors are encouraged to respect the plants and wildlife and to follow the garden's rules and guidelines to ensure a safe and enjoyable experience for all

The Dothan National Botanical Garden provides a beautiful and educational escape for families, offering a chance to connect with nature, learn about plants and conservation, and enjoy quality time together in a peaceful setting. With its diverse themed gardens, engaging educational programs, and family-friendly amenities, the botanical garden is a must-visit destination for families in the Dothan, Alabama area.

MONTE SANO
STATE PARK
ENJOY WALKING
HIKING AND BIKING
HONOR SYSTEM
ENTRY FEE 3.00

Monte Sano State Park

(Huntsville)

Address: 5105 Nolen Ave SE, Huntsville, AL 35801

Phone: (256) 534-3757

Hours: Park grounds open daily from sunrise to sunset

Admission: $5 per vehicle

Monte Sano State Park is an excellent destination for families looking to spend time outdoors, enjoying nature and participating in various recreational activities. With its diverse landscape, rich history, and range of amenities, the park offers something for visitors of all ages.

Activities and attractions for different age groups:

1. Toddlers and young children:
   - Exploring the park's easier hiking trails with their families, such as the Monte Sano Overlook Trail or the CCC Bike Trail
   - Enjoying picnics in the designated picnic areas or playgrounds
   - Participating in family-friendly events or nature programs offered by the park
2. Older children and teenagers:
   - Hiking the more challenging trails, such as the Stone Cuts Trail or the Natural Well Trail, to discover unique rock formations and scenic views
   - Biking on the park's mountain biking trails, which range from beginner to advanced levels

- ○ Playing disc golf on the park's 18-hole course
- ○ Attending ranger-led programs or workshops to learn about the park's ecology and history

3. Adults:
- ○ Hiking or trail running on the park's extensive network of trails, enjoying the scenic beauty and fresh air
- ○ Camping in the park's campgrounds, which offer both primitive and modern sites
- ○ Visiting the CCC Museum to learn about the park's history and the role of the Civilian Conservation Corps
- ○ Enjoying a relaxing picnic or barbecue in the designated picnic areas
- ○ Participating in volunteer opportunities, such as trail maintenance or habitat restoration projects

Amenities:

- The park offers several picnic areas with tables and grills, perfect for family gatherings or meals
- Campgrounds provide both primitive tent sites and modern RV sites with full hookups
- Restrooms and drinking water fountains are available throughout the park
- The Camp Store sells basic supplies, snacks, and souvenirs
- Free parking is available at various locations within the park

Handicap accessibility: Monte Sano State Park strives to provide an accessible experience for visitors with disabilities. The following accommodations are available:

- Some trails, such as the CCC Bike Trail and the Fossil Trail, are relatively flat and may be suitable for visitors with mobility issues
- The CCC Museum and some picnic areas are wheelchair accessible
- Handicap parking spaces are available at various locations throughout the park
- Service animals are welcome in the park

Stroller accessibility: Due to the nature of the park's terrain, many of the hiking trails are not suitable for strollers. However, some of the easier trails, such as the CCC Bike Trail or the Fossil Trail, may be navigable with a sturdy, all-terrain stroller. Families with young children may find it more convenient to use child carriers for hiking.

Other important information for visiting families:

- The park is open year-round, but some facilities and amenities may have seasonal hours or closures
- Some trails may be closed due to weather conditions or maintenance, so it's a good idea to check the park's website or contact the park office for the most up-to-date information
- Visitors should wear appropriate footwear and bring plenty of water and snacks for hiking or outdoor activities
- Families should be aware of park rules and regulations, such as properly disposing of waste, keeping pets on leashes, and respecting wildlife

Monte Sano State Park is a hidden gem for families seeking outdoor adventure, natural beauty, and a chance to disconnect from the distractions of daily life. With its wide range of activities, educational opportunities, and amenities, the park provides a memorable experience for visitors of all ages, fostering a deep appreciation for the great outdoors and the importance of preserving our natural heritage.

Guntersville Lake

(Northeast Alabama)

Address: Guntersville, AL 35976

Phone: (256) 571-7212 (Guntersville Lake Visitors Center)

Hours: Open 24/7

Admission: Free

Guntersville Lake is a fantastic destination for families looking to enjoy a variety of water-based activities and outdoor recreation. With its stunning scenery, diverse wildlife, and numerous amenities, the lake offers something for visitors of all ages.

Activities and attractions for different age groups:

1. Toddlers and young children:
     - Playing on the beaches and splashing in the shallow water along the shoreline
     - Enjoying picnics and family gatherings in the lakeside parks and picnic areas
     - Observing wildlife, such as birds and turtles, from the shore or during gentle boat rides
2. Older children and teenagers:
     - Swimming, kayaking, or paddleboarding in the lake's calm waters
     - Fishing for bass, crappie, or catfish from the shore, a pier, or a boat (with proper licenses)
     - Exploring the lake's coves and inlets on a rented pontoon boat or canoe
     - Hiking or biking on trails in the nearby parks and

nature reserves

3. Adults:
    ◦ Boating, water-skiing, or jet-skiing on the lake's expansive waters
    ◦ Fishing for trophy-sized bass or participating in fishing tournaments
    ◦ Relaxing on the beach or in the lakeside parks, soaking up the sun and scenery
    ◦ Enjoying a scenic drive around the lake, stopping at viewpoints and charming lakeside towns
    ◦ Golfing at one of the nearby golf courses with stunning lake views

Amenities:

- Several marinas around the lake offer boat rentals, fishing supplies, and other water-related amenities
- Numerous public boat launches provide easy access to the lake for those bringing their own boats
- Lakeside parks and campgrounds offer picnic areas, grills, restrooms, and sometimes playgrounds
- Some parks and campgrounds also provide swimming beaches, fishing piers, and hiking trails
- Nearby towns, such as Guntersville and Scottsboro, offer a variety of dining, shopping, and lodging options

Handicap accessibility: Accessibility at Guntersville Lake may vary depending on the specific location and facility. However, some general accommodations include:

- Many lakeside parks and campgrounds have paved pathways and accessible restrooms
- Some marinas and boat rental facilities may have accessible

docks or boat launches

- Fishing piers at some parks may be wheelchair accessible
- It's always best to contact the specific park, campground, or facility to inquire about their specific accessibility features

Stroller accessibility: Stroller accessibility around Guntersville Lake will depend on the specific location and terrain. Some considerations include:

- Many lakeside parks and campgrounds have paved or well-maintained paths suitable for strollers
- Beach areas may have sandy or uneven surfaces that can be challenging for strollers
- Some hiking trails may not be suitable for strollers due to rugged terrain or stairs
- Families with strollers should check with the specific park or facility for more information on stroller-friendly areas

Other important information for visiting families:

- Life jackets are essential for all water activities, especially for young children and inexperienced swimmers
- Sunscreen, hats, and insect repellent are recommended for outdoor activities, particularly during the summer months
- Fishing licenses are required for anyone 16 years or older fishing in Guntersville Lake
- Visitors should be aware of and follow all posted rules and regulations regarding boating, fishing, and park usage
- Some facilities and amenities may have seasonal hours or be closed during certain times of the year, so it's always a good idea to check ahead

Guntersville Lake is a must-visit destination for families seeking outdoor adventure, relaxation, and quality time together in a beautiful natural setting. With its wide range of activities, amenities, and stunning scenery, the lake provides a memorable experience for visitors of all ages, fostering a love for nature and a deep appreciation for the great outdoors.

Cathedral Caverns State Park

(Woodville)

Address: 637 Cave Rd, Woodville, AL 35776

Phone: (256) 728-8193

Hours: Park grounds open daily from 8 AM to 6 PM, Cave tours run hourly Admission: Adults $20, Children (6-11) $10, Children under 6 free

Cathedral Caverns State Park is an incredible destination for families looking to explore the wonders of the underground world and enjoy outdoor activities in a beautiful natural setting. With its massive caverns, stunning formations, and variety of amenities, the park offers a unique and memorable experience for visitors of all ages.

Activities and attractions for different age groups:

1. Toddlers and young children:
    - Participating in the guided cave tours, marveling at the colorful lights and unique formations (children under 6 are free)
    - Exploring the park's easy walking trails and nature paths under close adult supervision
    - Enjoying picnics and family gatherings in the park's picnic areas
2. Older children and teenagers:
    - Learning about the geology and history of the caverns during the guided tours
    - Participating in the GeoJourney program, an educational scavenger hunt through the caverns (additional fee required)

- Hiking the park's more challenging trails, such as the Pigeon Mountain Trail or the Tanyard Springs Trail
- Camping in the park's campground, enjoying evening campfires and stargazing

3. Adults:

- Marveling at the awe-inspiring formations and massive rooms during the guided cave tours
- Photographing the unique and stunning underground landscapes (camera flash allowed)
- Hiking or trail running on the park's various trails, enjoying the scenic views and fresh air
- Relaxing in the picnic areas or campgrounds, enjoying quality time with family and friends

Amenities:

- The park offers a campground with both primitive tent sites and RV sites with water and electrical hookups
- Picnic areas with tables and grills are available throughout the park
- A gift shop at the park entrance sells souvenirs, snacks, and beverages
- Restrooms and drinking water fountains are available near the cave entrance and in the campground
- Free parking is available at the park entrance and near the cave tour departure area

Handicap accessibility: Cathedral Caverns State Park strives to provide an accessible experience for visitors with disabilities. The following accommodations are available:

- The cave tour path is wheelchair accessible, with a flat,

paved surface and handrails in some areas

- Handicap parking spaces are available near the cave entrance and in the campground
- The park's picnic areas and restrooms are wheelchair accessible
- Service animals are welcome on the cave tours and in the park

Stroller accessibility: The cave tour path is stroller-friendly, with a flat, paved surface suitable for most strollers. However, some families may find it easier to carry infants or use a baby carrier during the tour. The park's easy walking trails and picnic areas are also generally stroller-accessible.

Other important information for visiting families:

- Cave tours run hourly from 10 AM to 4 PM, with extended hours during the summer months
- Reservations for cave tours are recommended, especially during peak season and on weekends
- The temperature inside the caverns remains a constant 60°F (15.5°C) year-round, so visitors should bring a light jacket or sweater
- Comfortable, closed-toe shoes with good traction are recommended for the cave tours and hiking trails
- Visitors should follow all park rules and regulations, including staying on designated trails and not touching or disturbing the cave formations

Cathedral Caverns State Park is a must-visit destination for families seeking adventure, education, and a unique experience in the heart of Alabama. With its awe-inspiring caverns, diverse outdoor activities, and family-friendly amenities, the park provides a memorable and enriching experience for visitors of all ages, fostering a deep appreciation for the natural wonders that lie beneath the Earth's surface.

Hippie Hole

(Hytop)

Address: County Road 521, Hytop, AL 35905

Phone: N/A

Hours: Open during daylight hours

Admission: Free

The Hippie Hole is a fantastic destination for families looking to escape the summer heat and enjoy a unique outdoor experience. With its natural beauty, refreshing waters, and opportunities for adventure, the Hippie Hole offers a memorable day trip for visitors of all ages.

Activities and attractions for different age groups:

1. Toddlers and young children:
    - Splashing and playing in the shallow areas of the swimming hole under close adult supervision
    - Exploring the surrounding rocks and nature, discovering small creatures and plant life
    - Enjoying picnics and family time on the rocks or in nearby shaded areas
2. Older children and teenagers:
    - Swimming and diving into the deeper parts of the swimming hole (with appropriate safety precautions)
    - Climbing and exploring the surrounding rock formations (with proper gear and adult supervision)

- ○ Taking part in water games and activities, such as water tag or Marco Polo
- ○ Capturing the beauty of the area through photography or nature sketching

3. Adults:

- ○ Relaxing and unwinding in the tranquil atmosphere of the Hippie Hole
- ○ Swimming and enjoying the cool, refreshing waters
- ○ Sunbathing on the warm rocks surrounding the swimming hole
- ○ Exploring the nearby hiking trails and taking in the scenic views of the area

Amenities:

- There are no formal amenities at the Hippie Hole, as it is a natural, undeveloped area
- Visitors should bring their own essentials, such as water, snacks, sunscreen, and first-aid supplies
- Parking is available along the roadside near the Hippie Hole, but space may be limited during peak times

Handicap accessibility: The Hippie Hole is a natural, rugged area and may not be easily accessible for individuals with mobility issues. The rocky terrain and lack of paved pathways may make it challenging for wheelchairs or those with limited mobility to access the swimming hole.

Stroller accessibility: Due to the rugged terrain and natural setting, the Hippie Hole is not well-suited for strollers. Families with young children may find it easier to carry their children or use baby carriers when visiting the area.

Other important information for visiting families:

- The Hippie Hole can be busy during peak summer months, so arriving early or visiting on weekdays may provide a more secluded experience
- There are no lifeguards on duty, so parents must closely supervise their children and ensure they are wearing appropriate safety gear, such as life jackets, when necessary
- Visitors should be aware of the potential for slippery rocks and exercise caution when climbing or diving
- As with any natural area, visitors should practice Leave No Trace principles, packing out all trash and leaving the area as they found it
- Visitors should also be prepared for changing weather conditions and bring appropriate clothing and gear

The Hippie Hole is a unique and refreshing destination for families looking to immerse themselves in nature and enjoy a memorable outdoor experience. While the lack of formal amenities may not suit everyone, those willing to embrace the rugged beauty and come prepared will find the Hippie Hole a delightful escape from the everyday. By following safety guidelines and respecting the natural environment, families can create lasting memories at this hidden gem in Hytop, Alabama.

Noccalula Falls Park

(Gadsden)

Address: 1500 Noccalula Rd, Gadsden, AL 35904

Phone: (256) 549-4663

Hours: Park grounds open daily from 7 AM to Sunset

Admission: $6 per vehicle

Noccalula Falls Park is a must-visit destination for families looking to experience the beauty of nature, enjoy outdoor activities, and learn about the area's history. With its stunning waterfall, diverse attractions, and family-friendly amenities, the park offers a memorable experience for visitors of all ages.

Activities and attractions for different age groups:

1. Toddlers and young children:
    - Enjoying the view of the majestic Noccalula Falls from the accessible observation deck
    - Visiting the petting zoo to interact with friendly animals like goats, sheep, and rabbits
    - Riding the miniature train that winds through the park, offering scenic views of the falls and surrounding area
2. Older children and teenagers:
    - Hiking the park's trails, which range from easy to moderate difficulty, to explore the natural beauty of the area
    - Learning about the area's history and early settler life at the pioneer village, which features

                 authentic, restored buildings
- Playing mini-golf at the park's 18-hole course, which offers a fun and challenging activity for the whole family
- Fishing in Black Creek (with proper licenses) or enjoying a picnic in the designated areas

3. Adults:
- Photographing the stunning Noccalula Falls from various viewpoints and trails
- Exploring the botanical gardens, which showcase diverse plant life and offer a peaceful retreat
- Attending one of the park's annual events or festivals, such as the Christmas at the Falls light display or the Smoke on the Falls BBQ competition
- Camping overnight in the park's campgrounds, which offer both RV and tent sites in a beautiful natural setting

Amenities:

- The park offers several picnic areas with tables and grills, perfect for family gatherings or meals
- Restrooms and drink machines are available throughout the park
- The campground provides RV sites with electrical and water hookups, as well as primitive tent sites
- A gift shop sells souvenirs, snacks, and beverages
- Free parking is available at various locations within the park

Handicap accessibility: Noccalula Falls Park strives to provide an accessible experience for visitors with disabilities. The following accommodations are available:

- The main observation deck overlooking the falls is wheelchair accessible
- Some of the park's trails, such as the Gorge Trail, are paved and relatively flat, making them easier to navigate for visitors with mobility issues
- Handicap parking spaces are available at various locations throughout the park
- The park's restrooms are ADA-compliant

Stroller accessibility: Many of the park's paved trails and walkways are stroller-friendly, making it easier for families with young children to explore the area. However, some of the more rugged hiking trails may not be suitable for strollers. Families should assess the difficulty of each trail before attempting to bring a stroller.

Other important information for visiting families:

- The park is open year-round, but some attractions and amenities may have seasonal hours or closures
- Swimming is not permitted in the waterfall or the creek due to safety concerns
- Pets are allowed in the park but must be kept on a leash at all times
- Visitors should follow all posted rules and regulations, such as properly disposing of waste and respecting wildlife
- In case of emergencies, visitors should contact park staff or call 911

Noccalula Falls Park is a gem for families seeking outdoor adventure, natural beauty, and a chance to create lasting memories together. With its iconic waterfall, diverse attractions, and family-friendly amenities, the park provides a well-rounded experience that caters to visitors of all ages and interests. By exploring the trails, learning about the area's history, and simply enjoying the stunning surroundings, families will find Noccalula Falls Park a rewarding and unforgettable destination in Gadsden, Alabama.

Birmingham Zoo

(Birmingham)

Address: 2630 Cahaba Rd, Birmingham, AL 35223

Phone: (205) 879-0409

Hours: Daily from 9 AM to 5 PM (Closed Thanksgiving and Christmas Day) Admission: Adults $19, Children (2-12) $14, Seniors (65+) $16

The Birmingham Zoo is an excellent destination for families looking to explore the wonders of the animal kingdom, learn about conservation, and enjoy a fun-filled day together. With its diverse exhibits, interactive experiences, and educational programs, the zoo offers something for visitors of all ages.

Activities and attractions for different age groups:

1. Toddlers and young children:
    - Visiting the Children's Zoo area, which features a petting zoo, interactive animal encounters, and age-appropriate play areas
    - Riding the Conservation Carousel or the Zoo Express Train for a fun and memorable experience
    - Attending animal feeding demonstrations or keeper talks to learn more about the animals in a kid-friendly way
2. Older children and teenagers:
    - Exploring the various animal exhibits, such as the Trails of Africa, Primate House, and Reptile House, to learn about different species and their habitats

- ○ Participating in educational programs, such as Zoo Camps or Animal Encounters, to gain a deeper understanding of animal behavior and conservation efforts
- ○ Enjoying the zoo's seasonal events, like Boo at the Zoo during Halloween or ZooLight Safari during the holiday season

3. Adults:
   - ○ Observing the diverse array of animals from around the world and learning about their unique characteristics and behaviors
   - ○ Attending keeper talks and animal demonstrations to gain insights into animal care and conservation efforts
   - ○ Supporting the zoo's conservation initiatives by making donations or adopting an animal
   - ○ Relaxing in the zoo's beautifully landscaped gardens and picnic areas

Amenities:

- The zoo offers several dining options, including the Kudzoo Café, Elephant's Trunk Pizza, and various snack kiosks throughout the park
- Gift shops sell souvenirs, toys, and animal-related merchandise
- Stroller and wheelchair rentals are available at the zoo entrance
- Restrooms and changing facilities are located throughout the zoo
- Free parking is available in the zoo's parking lot

Handicap accessibility: The Birmingham Zoo strives to provide an accessible experience for visitors with disabilities. The following accommodations are available:

- The zoo's paths are wheelchair accessible, with ramps and handrails in certain areas
- Wheelchair and electric scooter rentals are available at the zoo entrance
- Many of the animal exhibits have accessible viewing areas
- The zoo's restrooms are ADA-compliant
- Sign language interpreters can be provided for animal demonstrations and educational programs with advance notice

Stroller accessibility: The Birmingham Zoo is stroller-friendly, with wide, paved paths throughout the park. Stroller rentals are available at the zoo entrance for families who prefer not to bring their own.

Other important information for visiting families:

- The zoo is open year-round, but some exhibits and attractions may have seasonal closures or limited hours
- Visitors can purchase tickets online in advance to save time at the entrance
- The zoo offers a variety of membership options, which can provide discounts on admission, gift shop purchases, and special events
- Certain animal encounters and experiences, such as giraffe feedings and camel rides, require an additional fee
- The zoo has a strict no-smoking policy, and outside food and beverages are not permitted (except for water and special dietary needs)

The Birmingham Zoo is a must-visit attraction for families in the metropolitan Birmingham area. With its commitment to animal care, conservation, and education, the zoo provides a fun and enriching experience that fosters a love and appreciation for the natural world. By offering a wide range of exhibits, activities, and amenities, the Birmingham Zoo ensures that families of all ages and abilities can enjoy a memorable day together while learning about the incredible diversity of life on Earth.

McWane Science Center

(Birmingham)

Address: 200 19th St N, Birmingham, AL 35203

Phone: (205) 714-8300

Hours: Monday-Friday 9 AM-5 PM, Saturday 10 AM-6 PM, Sunday 12 PM-6 PM Admission: Adults $16, Children (2-12) $14, Seniors (65+) $14

The McWane Science Center is a fantastic destination for families seeking to explore the wonders of science, technology, and the natural world. With its hands-on exhibits, immersive experiences, and educational programs, the center provides an engaging and inspiring environment for visitors of all ages.

Activities and attractions for different age groups:

1. Toddlers and young children:
     - Exploring the Itty Bitty Magic City, a miniature town designed for children under six, where they can role-play various professions and learn about community life
     - Discovering the wonders of water play at the Just Mice Size exhibit, which features a water table and interactive elements
     - Enjoying the Sea Monsters exhibit, which showcases the fascinating world of prehistoric marine creatures through interactive displays and replica fossils
2. Older children and teenagers:
     - Discovering the principles of physics and

engineering at the Explore! exhibit, which features hands-on activities and demonstrations
- Learning about the human body and health at the BodyWorks exhibit, which includes interactive displays and a giant-sized replica of the human heart
- Experiencing the thrill of adventure sports at the High Cycle exhibit, where visitors can ride a bicycle along a wire suspended 20 feet above the ground
- Watching educational and entertaining films at the IMAX Dome Theater, which offers a unique and immersive viewing experience

3. Adults:
- Exploring the various exhibits alongside their children, fostering a love for science and learning
- Attending special events, such as Science Cocktail Nights or guest lectures, which offer engaging content tailored for adult audiences
- Participating in workshops and educational programs that cover a wide range of scientific topics and provide opportunities for hands-on learning

Amenities:

- The center features a café that offers a variety of snacks, meals, and beverages
- The Science Shop sells educational toys, books, and science-related souvenirs
- Lockers are available for rent to store personal belongings
- Restrooms and changing stations are located throughout the center

- Ample parking is available in nearby parking decks and lots

Handicap accessibility: The McWane Science Center is committed to providing an accessible and inclusive experience for all visitors. The following accommodations are available:

- The center's exhibits and facilities are wheelchair accessible, with ramps and elevators providing access to all levels
- Wheelchair rentals are available at the ticket desk on a first-come, first-served basis
- The IMAX Dome Theater offers accessible seating and assistive listening devices
- Service animals are welcome in the center
- The center's staff is trained to assist visitors with disabilities and provide accommodations as needed

Stroller accessibility: The McWane Science Center is stroller-friendly, with wide hallways and elevators that accommodate strollers. However, some exhibits may have limited space or require visitors to park their strollers in designated areas.

Other important information for visiting families:

- The center can be busy during weekends and school holidays, so it is recommended to arrive early or purchase tickets in advance online
- Some exhibits and activities may have height or age restrictions for safety reasons
- The center offers a variety of membership options, which can provide discounts on admission, IMAX tickets, and gift shop purchases
- Certain educational programs and workshops may require advance registration and additional fees

- The center enforces a strict no-smoking policy, and outside food and beverages are not permitted

The McWane Science Center is a must-visit destination for families in the Birmingham area who wish to explore the fascinating world of science and technology. With its engaging exhibits, immersive experiences, and commitment to accessibility, the center provides an unforgettable learning experience that sparks curiosity and encourages scientific discovery. By offering a wide range of activities and amenities, the McWane Science Center ensures that visitors of all ages and abilities can enjoy a fun-filled and educational day together.

Vulcan Park and Museum

(Birmingham)

Address: 1701 Valley View Dr, Birmingham, AL 35209

Phone: (205) 933-1409

Hours: Tuesday-Sunday 10 AM - 6 PM (Closed Mondays)

Admission: Adults $8, Children (5-12) $6, Children under 5 free

Vulcan Park and Museum is a fascinating destination that offers families a unique blend of history, culture, and outdoor recreation. With its iconic statue, informative exhibits, and scenic park setting, Vulcan Park and Museum provides an engaging and educational experience for visitors of all ages.

Activities and attractions for different age groups:

1. Toddlers and young children:
   - Enjoying the park's outdoor spaces, including the large lawn area perfect for running and playing
   - Participating in age-appropriate scavenger hunts or activity sheets provided by the museum
   - Attending special events and festivals that offer kid-friendly activities and entertainment
2. Older children and teenagers:
   - Exploring the museum's exhibits to learn about Birmingham's industrial history and the creation of the Vulcan statue
   - Climbing the observation tower to enjoy panoramic views of the city and surrounding areas
   - Participating in guided tours or educational

programs that delve deeper into the park's history and significance

- ◦ Engaging in outdoor activities, such as hiking the park's trails or enjoying a picnic on the grounds

3. Adults:
   - ◦ Admiring the impressive Vulcan statue and learning about its symbolic importance to Birmingham
   - ◦ Discovering the city's rich history and cultural heritage through the museum's exhibits and displays
   - ◦ Attending special events, such as concerts, festivals, or movie screenings, held at the park throughout the year
   - ◦ Enjoying the park's serene setting and taking in the beautiful views of the city skyline

Amenities:

- The Vulcan Center Museum Store offers a variety of souvenirs, books, and locally-made gifts
- Picnic tables and benches are located throughout the park for visitors to enjoy outdoor meals or relaxation
- Restrooms are available in the Vulcan Center and near the observation tower
- On-site parking is available for a fee, with discounts for museum visitors

Handicap accessibility: Vulcan Park and Museum strives to provide an accessible experience for all visitors. The following accommodations are available:

- The Vulcan Center, museum exhibits, and observation

tower are wheelchair accessible
- Handicap parking spaces are available in the on-site parking lot
- Assistive listening devices are available for guided tours and educational programs
- Service animals are welcome in the park and museum

Stroller accessibility: Vulcan Park and Museum is stroller-friendly, with paved paths throughout the park and ample space in the museum exhibits. However, strollers are not permitted on the observation deck due to safety concerns.

Other important information for visiting families:

- The park is open year-round, but the museum and observation tower may have different hours of operation
- Guided tours of the museum and park are available for an additional fee and require advance reservations
- The park hosts various events and festivals throughout the year, some of which may require separate tickets or reservations
- Visitors are encouraged to bring water and sunscreen, especially during the warmer months, as much of the park is outdoors
- The park and museum enforce a strict no-smoking policy, and outside food and beverages are not permitted inside the museum

Vulcan Park and Museum is a must-visit destination for families in the Birmingham area who want to explore the city's history, culture, and natural beauty. With its iconic statue, informative exhibits, and stunning views, the park offers a unique and memorable experience that combines education and recreation. By providing a range of activities, amenities, and accessibility features, Vulcan Park and Museum ensures that visitors of all ages and abilities can enjoy a fun and enriching day together while learning about Birmingham's fascinating past and vibrant present.

Birmingham Botanical Gardens

(Birmingham)

Address: 2612 Lane Park Rd, Birmingham, AL 35223

Phone: (205) 414-3950

Hours: Daily from 7 AM to 6 PM (Closed Thanksgiving and Christmas Day) Admission: Adults $18, Children (2-12) $12, Seniors (60+) $15

The Birmingham Botanical Gardens is a remarkable destination that offers families a beautiful and educational outdoor experience. With its diverse themed gardens, interactive exhibits, and engaging programs, the gardens provide a wonderful opportunity for visitors of all ages to connect with nature and learn about the world of plants.

Activities and attractions for different age groups:

1. Toddlers and young children:
    - Exploring the Children's Garden, which features interactive play areas, sensory gardens, and a splash pad
    - Participating in age-appropriate scavenger hunts or nature-themed activities provided by the gardens
    - Enjoying story time or kid-friendly tours led by the gardens' education staff
2. Older children and teenagers:
    - Discovering the diverse plant life and ecosystems represented in the various themed gardens
    - Learning about the importance of conservation

and sustainability through educational programs and workshops
- Participating in guided tours that delve deeper into the history, design, and significance of the gardens
- Exploring the gardens' walking trails and identifying plants and wildlife using guidebooks or smartphone apps

3. Adults:
- Admiring the beauty and serenity of the themed gardens, such as the Japanese Gardens or the Conservatory
- Attending gardening workshops, lectures, or classes to learn about plant care, landscaping, or floral design
- Participating in special events, such as the Spring Plant Sale or the Antiques at the Gardens show
- Enjoying a peaceful picnic or relaxing stroll through the gardens' tranquil settings

Amenities:

- The Gardens Café offers a variety of sandwiches, salads, and beverages for visitors to enjoy
- The Gift Shop sells plants, gardening supplies, books, and garden-themed souvenirs
- Restrooms and water fountains are located throughout the gardens
- Free parking is available in the gardens' parking lot

Handicap accessibility: The Birmingham Botanical Gardens is committed to providing an accessible experience for all visitors. The following accommodations are available:

- The majority of the gardens' paths are wheelchair accessible, with smooth, paved surfaces
- Wheelchair and electric scooter rentals are available at the front desk on a first-come, first-served basis
- Braille signage and audio tours are available for visually impaired visitors
- Service animals are welcome in the gardens

Stroller accessibility: The Birmingham Botanical Gardens is stroller-friendly, with wide, paved paths throughout the property. However, some areas, such as the Japanese Gardens, may have steps or narrow passages that could be challenging for strollers.

Other important information for visiting families:

- The gardens are open year-round, but some areas may be closed for maintenance or due to inclement weather
- Guided tours are available for an additional fee and require advance reservations
- The gardens host various events and workshops throughout the year, some of which may require separate tickets or reservations
- Visitors are encouraged to bring water, sunscreen, and insect repellent, especially during the warmer months
- The gardens enforce a strict no-smoking policy, and outside food and beverages are not permitted in the Gardens Café or during special events

The Birmingham Botanical Gardens is a must-visit destination for families who want to explore the beauty and diversity of the plant world while enjoying a peaceful and educational outdoor experience. With its stunning themed gardens, interactive children's area, and diverse range of programs and events, the gardens offer something for visitors of all ages and interests. By providing accessible paths, helpful amenities, and engaging learning opportunities, the Birmingham Botanical Gardens ensures that families can create lasting memories while cultivating a deeper appreciation for nature and the environment.

Red Mountain Park

(Birmingham)

Address: 2676 Terrace Crest Blvd, Birmingham, AL 35211

Phone: (205) 833-3451

Hours: Daily from 7 AM to 7 PM

Admission: Free (charges for some activities)

Red Mountain Park is an incredible destination for families seeking outdoor adventure, natural beauty, and a wide range of activities suitable for all ages. With its expansive trails, thrilling attractions, and scenic landscapes, the park offers an unforgettable experience that combines recreation, education, and family bonding.

Activities and attractions for different age groups:

1. Toddlers and young children:
    - Exploring the park's playgrounds and open green spaces, which provide ample room for running, playing, and picnicking
    - Participating in age-appropriate nature walks or scavenger hunts led by park rangers or educators
    - Enjoying family-friendly events, such as storytelling sessions or nature-themed crafts and activities
2. Older children and teenagers:
    - Hiking or biking the park's extensive trail system, which offers varying levels of difficulty and stunning views
    - Challenging themselves on the park's adventure

courses, such as the Kaul Adventure Tower or the Vulcan Materials Zip Trip
- Learning about the park's mining history and ecology through guided tours or educational programs
- Participating in team-building activities or outdoor skills workshops, such as orienteering or survival skills

3. Adults:
- Enjoying scenic hikes or trail runs on the park's diverse trails, ranging from easy nature walks to more strenuous routes
- Experiencing the thrill of the Red Ore Zip Tour, which offers breathtaking views and an adrenaline rush
- Attending outdoor fitness classes, such as yoga or boot camps, in the park's beautiful natural settings
- Participating in volunteer opportunities, such as trail maintenance or habitat restoration projects
- Relaxing in the park's picnic areas or open green spaces, soaking in the tranquil atmosphere

Amenities:

- The park offers several picnic areas with tables and grills, perfect for family gatherings or outdoor meals
- Restrooms and drinking fountains are located throughout the park
- A visitor center provides information, maps, and souvenirs for park guests
- Ample parking is available at various trailheads and attractions within the park

Handicap accessibility: Red Mountain Park strives to provide an accessible outdoor experience for visitors with disabilities. The following accommodations are available:

- Some trails, such as the BMRR South Trail and the Smythe Trail, are relatively flat and wide, making them more accessible for visitors with mobility issues
- The park's visitor center and some picnic areas are wheelchair accessible
- Handicap parking spaces are available at various locations throughout the park
- Service animals are welcome on the park's trails and attractions

Stroller accessibility: While Red Mountain Park is a natural setting with varied terrain, some trails and areas are more stroller-friendly than others. The BMRR South Trail and the Smythe Trail are relatively flat and wide, making them better suited for strollers. However, many of the park's trails and attractions may be challenging or inaccessible for strollers due to uneven surfaces, stairs, or narrow passages.

Other important information for visiting families:

- The park is open year-round, but some attractions and amenities may have seasonal hours or closures
- Some activities, such as the zip lines and adventure courses, have age, height, and weight restrictions for safety reasons
- Advance reservations may be required for certain activities or programs, so it's best to check the park's website or contact the visitor center for the most up-to-date information
- Visitors should wear appropriate footwear and bring

plenty of water, snacks, and sun protection, especially
during the warmer months

- The park enforces a "leave no trace" policy, asking visitors
  to properly dispose of waste and respect the natural
  environment

Red Mountain Park is a must-visit destination for families in the
Birmingham area who want to immerse themselves in nature,
challenge themselves with exciting outdoor activities, and create
lasting memories together. With its diverse range of attractions,
accessible amenities, and commitment to environmental education,
the park offers a unique and enriching experience that encourages
a love for the great outdoors and an appreciation for the region's
natural and cultural heritage.

Railroad Park

(Birmingham)

Address: 1600 1st Ave S, Birmingham, AL 35233

Phone: (205) 521-9933

Hours: Park grounds open daily from 7 AM to 11 PM

Admission: Free

Railroad Park is a wonderful urban oasis that offers families a delightful mix of outdoor recreation, relaxation, and community events. With its spacious green lawns, walking trails, and modern playground, the park provides a perfect setting for families to spend quality time together and enjoy the beauty of nature in the heart of the city.

Activities and attractions for different age groups:

1. Toddlers and young children:
    - Playing on the park's state-of-the-art playground, which features age-appropriate equipment and soft surfaces
    - Enjoying picnics or snack time on the park's lush green lawns
    - Participating in family-friendly events, such as storytelling sessions or children's concerts
2. Older children and teenagers:
    - Playing frisbee, tag, or other outdoor games on the park's expansive green spaces
    - Exploring the park's walking and jogging trails, which offer a chance to exercise and enjoy the

scenery
- Attending outdoor movie nights or concerts held at the park throughout the year
- Participating in community events, such as art workshops or fitness classes

3. Adults:
- Relaxing on the park's beautiful lawns, enjoying a picnic or a good book
- Walking, jogging, or cycling on the park's trails for exercise and fresh air
- Attending outdoor concerts, movie nights, or cultural events held at the park
- Enjoying the park's central location and proximity to other downtown attractions, restaurants, and shops

Amenities:

- The park features restrooms and water fountains for visitor convenience
- Benches and seating areas are located throughout the park for relaxation and enjoyment of the scenery
- Ample trash and recycling receptacles are provided to help keep the park clean and eco-friendly
- Free Wi-Fi is available in some areas of the park

Handicap accessibility: Railroad Park is committed to providing an accessible and inclusive outdoor experience for all visitors. The following accommodations are available:

- The park's paths and trails are wheelchair accessible, with smooth, paved surfaces and gentle inclines
- Handicap parking spaces are available in the nearby

parking areas
- The park's restrooms are ADA-compliant and accessible for visitors with disabilities
- Service animals are welcome in the park

Stroller accessibility: Railroad Park is stroller-friendly, with wide, paved paths and trails that are easy to navigate with strollers. The park's level terrain and smooth surfaces make it a comfortable and convenient destination for families with young children in strollers.

Other important information for visiting families:

- The park is open daily from 7 AM to 11 PM, providing ample opportunity for families to visit and enjoy the space
- Parking is available in nearby lots and garages, some of which may require a fee
- The park hosts various events and activities throughout the year, so it's a good idea to check the park's website or social media for the most up-to-date information
- Visitors are encouraged to follow park rules and guidelines, such as properly disposing of waste, respecting other visitors, and keeping dogs on leashes
- The park is a smoke-free environment, and alcohol is not permitted without special permission

Railroad Park is a must-visit destination for families in the Birmingham area who want to enjoy a beautiful, accessible, and engaging outdoor space in the heart of the city. With its diverse amenities, community events, and central location, the park offers a unique and enjoyable experience that promotes healthy living, family bonding, and a sense of community. By providing a welcoming and inclusive environment for visitors of all ages and abilities, Railroad Park serves as a vibrant gathering place and a source of pride for the people of Birmingham.

Birmingham Civil Rights Institute

(Birmingham)

Address: 520 16th St N, Birmingham, AL 35203

Phone: (205) 328-9696

Hours: Tuesday-Saturday 10 AM - 5 PM, Sunday 1 PM - 5 PM (Closed Mondays)

Admission: Adults $15, Children (4-17) $8, Seniors (65+) $12

The Birmingham Civil Rights Institute is an essential destination for families who want to learn about the history of the Civil Rights Movement and its enduring impact on American society. With its thought-provoking exhibits, educational programs, and powerful artifacts, the institute provides a deeply meaningful and transformative experience for visitors of all ages.

Activities and attractions for different age groups:

1. Elementary school-aged children (6-12):
    - Exploring the "Kids' Corner" exhibit, which offers age-appropriate activities and resources to help children understand the Civil Rights Movement
    - Participating in guided tours designed specifically for young learners, which use storytelling and interactive elements to engage children
    - Attending special events and workshops, such as the "Kids in the Kitchen" program, which combines cooking and learning about civil rights history
2. Teenagers (13-17):

- Engaging with the museum's main exhibits, which offer a comprehensive and thought-provoking look at the history of the Civil Rights Movement
- Participating in youth-focused educational programs, such as the "Youth Docent" program, which trains students to lead tours and share their knowledge with others
- Attending panel discussions, lectures, and film screenings that explore contemporary civil rights issues and their historical context

3. Adults:
   - Immersing themselves in the museum's rich collection of artifacts, photographs, and multimedia displays that bring the history of the Civil Rights Movement to life
   - Attending lectures, workshops, and special events that delve deeper into specific aspects of civil rights history and contemporary social justice issues
   - Engaging in personal reflection and dialogue with others about the ongoing struggle for equality and justice in American society

Amenities:

- The museum's gift shop offers a wide selection of books, souvenirs, and educational resources related to civil rights history
- Restrooms and water fountains are available for visitor convenience
- Limited parking is available in nearby lots and garages, some of which may require a fee

Handicap accessibility: The Birmingham Civil Rights Institute is committed to providing an accessible and inclusive experience for all visitors. The following accommodations are available:

- The museum is fully wheelchair accessible, with elevators and ramps providing access to all exhibits and facilities
- Wheelchairs are available for loan at the museum's front desk on a first-come, first-served basis
- Assistive listening devices and audio descriptions are available for select exhibits and programs
- Sign language interpretation can be arranged for tours and events with advance notice
- Service animals are welcome in the museum

Stroller accessibility: The Birmingham Civil Rights Institute is stroller-friendly, with wide, level pathways and elevators that accommodate strollers. However, some exhibit areas may be more crowded or have limited space, so families with strollers should be prepared to navigate carefully or park their strollers in designated areas if needed.

Other important information for visiting families:

- The museum is closed on Mondays and major holidays, so it's important to plan your visit accordingly
- Guided tours are available for an additional fee and can be reserved in advance through the museum's website or by phone
- The museum hosts special events and temporary exhibitions throughout the year, so it's a good idea to check the museum's website or social media for the most up-to-date information
- Photography is permitted in most areas of the museum,

but visitors should be respectful of others and refrain from using flash in certain exhibit areas

- The museum has a strict policy prohibiting food, drinks, and large bags in the exhibit areas to help preserve the artifacts and maintain a safe and comfortable environment for all visitors

The Birmingham Civil Rights Institute is a vital educational resource and a testament to the courage and resilience of those who fought for civil rights in America. By engaging visitors of all ages with its powerful exhibits, educational programs, and commitment to accessibility and inclusion, the institute ensures that the lessons of the past continue to inform and inspire future generations in the ongoing struggle for social justice and equality.

Alabama Splash Adventure

(Bessemer)

Address: 4599 Adventure Trail, Bessemer, AL 35022

Phone: (205) 481-4750

Hours: Seasonal hours, typically open from late May to early August

Admission: General admission prices vary, but typically around $30 for adults and $25 for children (under 48 inches tall)

Alabama Splash Adventure is a fantastic destination for families looking to enjoy a fun-filled day of water activities, thrilling rides, and outdoor entertainment. With its wide range of attractions catering to different ages and interests, the park offers an exciting and memorable experience for the whole family.

Activities and attractions for different age groups:

1. Toddlers and young children:
   - Exploring the Castaway Island area, which features smaller slides, splash pads, and water play structures designed for younger children
   - Enjoying the Salamander Bay and Turtle Reef attractions, which offer gentle water slides and shallow pools for little ones
   - Participating in the park's "Kiddie Korral" program, which provides supervised activities and games for children aged 4-7
2. Older children and teenagers:
   - Experiencing the thrilling water slides, such as the Rampage, Acapulco Drop, and Splashdown,

which offer high-speed adventures and steep drops
  - Challenging themselves on the park's racing slides, like the Cyclone Racer and Neptune's Plunge
  - Enjoying the Kahuna Waves, a massive 800,000-gallon wave pool that simulates ocean waves
  - Relaxing and floating along the Warrior River, a lazy river that winds through the park

3. Adults:
  - Accompanying their children on family-friendly attractions like the Warrior River and the Kahuna Waves
  - Relaxing in the park's cabanas or shaded seating areas while supervising their children
  - Enjoying food and beverages from the park's various dining options, including the Ohana BBQ & Grill and the Tiki Bar
  - Shopping for souvenirs and essentials at the park's gift shops

Amenities:

- The park offers several dining options, from quick snacks to full meals, including burgers, pizza, BBQ, and ice cream
- Cabanas and lounge chairs are available for rent, providing a private and shaded space for families to relax
- Lockers and changing rooms are available for a fee, allowing visitors to store their belongings and change in and out of swimwear
- Free parking is available on-site, with designated areas for buses and RVs

Handicap accessibility: Alabama Splash Adventure strives to provide an accessible and enjoyable experience for all guests. The following accommodations are available:

- The park is wheelchair accessible, with ramps and paved pathways connecting the main attractions and facilities
- Some water attractions, such as the Warrior River and the Salamander Bay, are accessible for guests with limited mobility
- Handicap parking spaces are available near the park entrance
- Service animals are welcome in the park, but may be restricted from certain water attractions for safety reasons

Stroller accessibility: Alabama Splash Adventure is stroller-friendly, with paved pathways and ample space for navigating the park with strollers. However, strollers may not be allowed in certain queue lines or on water attractions for safety reasons. The park offers stroller parking areas near the main attractions, allowing families to safely store their strollers while enjoying the rides.

Other important information for visiting families:

- The park is open seasonally, typically from late May to early August, so it's essential to check the park's website or social media for the most up-to-date operating hours and dates
- Height and weight restrictions apply to some water attractions, so it's important to review the park's policies and guidelines before visiting
- Outside food and beverages are not permitted inside the park, but picnic areas are available outside the main entrance for families who wish to bring their own meals
- Visitors are encouraged to apply sunscreen regularly and

stay hydrated throughout their visit, as the park is primarily outdoors and can get very hot during the summer months
- The park may close certain attractions or limit operating hours due to inclement weather or other unforeseen circumstances, so it's a good idea to check the park's status before visiting

Alabama Splash Adventure is a must-visit destination for families seeking a thrilling and refreshing escape from the summer heat. With its diverse range of water attractions, family-friendly amenities, and commitment to accessibility, the park offers a fun and inclusive experience for visitors of all ages and abilities. By providing a safe and well-maintained environment for outdoor entertainment, Alabama Splash Adventure ensures that families can create lasting memories and enjoy a splashing good time together.

THE FOAM PIT

Airwalk Trampoline Park

(Hoover)

Address: 5480 Stadium Trace Pkwy, Hoover, AL 35244

Phone: (205) 408-3222

Hours: Monday-Thursday 10 AM - 8 PM, Friday-Saturday 10 AM - 10 PM, Sunday 12 PM - 8 PM

Admission: Prices vary based on activity and time, but typically around $15-$20 for 1-hour jump pass

Airwalk Trampoline Park is an exciting indoor destination that offers a wide range of activities for families with children of all ages. With its emphasis on active play, physical fitness, and fun, the park provides a unique and engaging experience that encourages children to explore their abilities and challenge themselves in a safe and controlled environment.

Activities and attractions for different age groups:

1. Toddlers and young children (1-5):
    - Exploring the dedicated Toddler Zone, which features smaller trampolines and soft play structures designed for the safety and enjoyment of younger children
    - Participating in parent-assisted jumping sessions, where parents can accompany their little ones on the trampolines
    - Enjoying the park's foam pits, which provide a soft and safe landing for young jumpers
2. Elementary school-aged children (6-12):

- ◦ Jumping and flipping on the main trampoline area, which offers over 10,000 square feet of interconnected trampolines
- ◦ Playing trampoline dodgeball, basketball, or participating in the trampoline-infused obstacle course
- ◦ Challenging themselves on the park's ninja warrior course, which features a variety of obstacles and challenges to test agility and strength
- ◦ Participating in supervised jumping sessions and organized games led by the park's trained staff
3. Teenagers (13-17):
    - ◦ Mastering advanced flips, tricks, and techniques on the main trampoline area or in the designated trick zones
    - ◦ Competing with friends in trampoline dodgeball tournaments or basketball games
    - ◦ Attending special events, such as glow-in-the-dark jumping sessions or teen-only nights
    - ◦ Improving their fitness and coordination through regular trampoline exercise and play

Amenities:

- The park offers a viewing area for parents and non-jumping guests, complete with comfortable seating and free Wi-Fi
- Lockers are available for rent, allowing visitors to securely store their belongings while enjoying the park
- The park has a concession area that serves snacks, drinks, and light meals
- Air conditioning throughout the facility ensures a comfortable environment for jumping and playing

Safety and accessibility: Airwalk Trampoline Park prioritizes safety and strives to create an inclusive environment for all guests. The following measures are in place:

- All jumpers must complete a safety waiver and watch a brief safety video before participating
- The park employs trained staff to supervise jumping areas and ensure that guests follow safety guidelines
- Jumpers are grouped by age and size to promote a safe and enjoyable experience for everyone
- The Toddler Zone is separated from the main jumping areas to ensure the safety of younger children
- The park is wheelchair accessible, with ramps and wide pathways for easy navigation

Birthday parties and special events: Airwalk Trampoline Park is a popular destination for birthday parties and special events. The park offers a variety of party packages that include private jumping time, dedicated party hosts, and access to private party rooms. The park can also accommodate group events, such as field trips, team-building activities, and fundraisers.

Other important information for visiting families:

- Socks are required for all jumpers and can be purchased at the park if needed
- Jumpers should wear comfortable, athletic clothing and remove all jewelry and sharp objects before jumping
- Outside food and drinks are not permitted in the park, but guests may bring water bottles
- Waivers must be signed by a parent or legal guardian for all jumpers under the age of 18
- The park offers special discounts and promotions

throughout the year, so it's a good idea to check their website or social media for the latest offers

Airwalk Trampoline Park is a must-visit destination for families seeking a fun, active, and engaging indoor experience. With its diverse range of attractions, commitment to safety, and inclusive atmosphere, the park offers a memorable and exciting day out for children and adults alike. Whether you're looking to host a birthday party, improve your fitness, or simply have a great time with family and friends, Airwalk Trampoline Park in Hoover is sure to provide an unforgettable experience.

Oak Mountain State Park

(Pelham)

Address: 200 Terrace Dr, Pelham, AL 35124

Phone: (205) 620-2520

Hours: Park grounds open daily from sunrise to sunset

Admission: $5 per vehicle

Oak Mountain State Park is an incredible destination for families who love outdoor adventures and natural beauty. With its expansive size, diverse landscapes, and wide range of activities, the park offers something for everyone, making it an ideal spot for family getaways, day trips, and weekend camping excursions.

Activities and attractions for different age groups:

1. Toddlers and young children:
    - Exploring the park's easy nature trails and boardwalks, such as the Treetop Nature Trail or the Peavine Falls Boardwalk
    - Playing at the park's playgrounds, which offer age-appropriate equipment and safe surfaces
    - Enjoying picnics and family gatherings at the park's many picnic areas, some of which have grills and shelters
2. Elementary school-aged children:
    - Hiking on the park's more challenging trails, such as the White Trail or the Blue Trail, to discover waterfalls, streams, and scenic overlooks
    - Participating in the park's educational programs,

such as guided nature walks or wildlife presentations
- Fishing in the park's lakes, which are stocked with bass, bream, and catfish (fishing license required for ages 12 and up)
- Swimming in the park's beach area at Double Oak Lake, which features a sandy beach, diving boards, and a water slide

3. Teenagers:
- Mountain biking on the park's extensive trail system, which includes over 30 miles of trails suitable for various skill levels
- Participating in the park's archery or BMX racing programs, which offer instruction and equipment rentals
- Horseback riding on the park's equestrian trails, with guided trail rides available through the stables
- Joining the park's Ranger-led programs, such as the Oak Mountain Interpretive Center's "Snake Encounter" or "Owl Prowl"

Amenities:

- The park offers several campgrounds, including primitive tent sites, RV sites with hookups, and cabin rentals
- Picnic areas throughout the park provide tables, grills, and sometimes shelters for family gatherings
- The park's beach area at Double Oak Lake features restrooms, showers, and a concession stand
- The park has a golf pro shop, a BMX track, and an equestrian center that offer equipment rentals and instruction

- The park's Interpretive Center features exhibits on the park's natural history, wildlife, and ecology

Safety and accessibility: Oak Mountain State Park strives to provide a safe and accessible outdoor experience for all visitors. The following measures are in place:

- The park's main facilities, such as restrooms, picnic areas, and the beach, are wheelchair accessible
- Some of the park's trails, such as the Treetop Nature Trail and the Peavine Falls Boardwalk, are accessible for visitors with mobility issues
- The park's staff is trained in first aid and CPR, and emergency services are available in case of accidents or injuries
- Visitors are encouraged to follow park rules and guidelines, such as staying on designated trails, properly disposing of waste, and respecting wildlife

Other important information for visiting families:

- The park is open year-round, but some facilities and activities may have seasonal hours or closures
- A valid Alabama fishing license is required for fishing in the park's lakes, and size and catch limits apply
- Some activities, such as horseback riding, BMX racing, and golf, may require additional fees or reservations
- The park hosts various events throughout the year, such as the Oak Mountain State Fair, the Hummingbird Festival, and the Xterra off-road triathlon
- Visitors should bring plenty of water, snacks, and sun protection, especially during the summer months, and be prepared for changing weather conditions

Oak Mountain State Park is a must-visit destination for families who love the great outdoors and want to create unforgettable memories in a stunning natural setting. With its incredible range of activities, amenities, and educational opportunities, the park offers a truly immersive and enriching experience for visitors of all ages and interests. Whether you're seeking adventure, relaxation, or a chance to connect with nature, Oak Mountain State Park is sure to exceed your expectations and leave you with a deep appreciation for Alabama's natural wonders.

Montgomery Zoo

(Montgomery)

Address: 2940 Coliseum Pkwy, Montgomery, AL 36109

Phone: (334) 240-4900

Hours: Monday-Friday 9 AM - 5 PM, Saturday-Sunday 9 AM - 6 PM

Admission: Adults $17, Children (3-12) $12, Seniors (65+) $14

The Montgomery Zoo is a wonderful destination for families looking to explore the fascinating world of animals and learn about conservation efforts. With its diverse collection of species, interactive experiences, and educational programs, the zoo offers an engaging and memorable day out for visitors of all ages.

Activities and attractions for different age groups:

1. Toddlers and young children:
     - Observing and learning about the zoo's various animals, such as the playful monkeys, colorful birds, and majestic big cats
     - Enjoying the zoo's playground areas, which offer age-appropriate equipment and a chance to burn off extra energy
     - Participating in the zoo's "Little Critters" program, which provides special activities and experiences for children aged 2-5
2. Elementary school-aged children:
     - Attending the zoo's educational programs, such as the "Zoo School" or "Zoo Camp," which offer

- hands-on learning experiences and behind-the-scenes access
- Exploring the zoo's themed areas, such as the South American Exhibit or the African Exhibit, to learn about different habitats and ecosystems
- Participating in the zoo's scavenger hunts or guided tours, which encourage children to engage with the exhibits and learn fun facts about the animals

3. Teenagers:
- Attending the zoo's "Teen Keeper" program, which allows participants to work alongside zookeepers and learn about animal care and conservation
- Volunteering at the zoo through the "Teen Volunteer" program, which provides opportunities to assist with special events, education programs, and animal care
- Participating in the zoo's photography or art contests, which encourage creative expression and a deeper connection with the natural world

Amenities:

- The zoo offers several dining options, including the Overlook Cafe, which serves sandwiches, salads, and snacks
- Gift shops located throughout the zoo sell souvenirs, toys, and animal-related merchandise
- Strollers and wheelchairs are available for rent at the zoo's entrance
- The zoo provides several picnic areas for families who wish to bring their own food and enjoy a meal on the grounds

Safety and accessibility: The Montgomery Zoo is committed to providing a safe and accessible experience for all visitors. The following measures are in place:

- The zoo's paths are wheelchair accessible, and the zoo provides a limited number of wheelchairs for rent
- Safety barriers and signage are in place to ensure the well-being of both visitors and animals
- The zoo's staff is trained in first aid and emergency procedures, and first-aid stations are located throughout the park
- Visitors are encouraged to follow zoo rules and guidelines, such as not feeding the animals and staying on designated paths

Special experiences and events: The Montgomery Zoo offers several unique experiences and events throughout the year, including:

- The "Zoofari Skylift," a chairlift ride that provides aerial views of the zoo and its inhabitants
- The "Zoo Weekend" event series, which features special animal encounters, live music, and family-friendly activities
- The "Christmas Lights Festival," an annual holiday event that transforms the zoo into a winter wonderland with thousands of twinkling lights and festive displays

Other important information for visiting families:

- The zoo is open year-round, but some exhibits and attractions may have seasonal hours or closures
- Visitors can purchase tickets online in advance or at the zoo's entrance; discounts may be available for military personnel, seniors, and Montgomery residents

- The zoo offers membership packages that provide unlimited annual admission, discounts on special experiences, and other perks
- Visitors should bring comfortable walking shoes, sun protection, and insect repellent, especially during the warmer months

The Montgomery Zoo is a must-visit attraction for families in the Montgomery area and beyond. With its commitment to animal care, conservation education, and visitor engagement, the zoo provides a fun and meaningful experience that helps foster a lifelong love and respect for the natural world. Whether you're interested in observing fascinating creatures, learning about their habitats and behaviors, or simply enjoying a day outdoors with loved ones, the Montgomery Zoo is sure to create lasting memories and inspire a greater appreciation for the incredible diversity of life on Earth.

Old Alabama Town

(Montgomery)

Address: 301 Columbus St, Montgomery, AL 36104

Phone: (334) 240-4500

Hours: Tuesday-Saturday 10 AM - 4 PM, Sunday 1 PM - 4 PM (Closed Mondays)

Admission: Adults $10, Children (6-18) $6, Children under 6 free

Old Alabama Town is a fascinating destination that offers families a unique opportunity to step back in time and experience life in 19th-century Alabama. With its authentic buildings, costumed interpreters, and engaging living history demonstrations, the museum provides an immersive and educational experience for visitors of all ages.

Activities and attractions for different age groups:

1. Elementary school-aged children (6-12):
    - Exploring the museum's historic buildings, such as the one-room schoolhouse, the pioneer cabin, and the blacksmith shop
    - Interacting with costumed interpreters who demonstrate traditional crafts and trades, such as spinning, weaving, and candle-making
    - Participating in hands-on activities and games that were popular during the 19th century, such as hoop rolling and marbles
    - Attending special events, like the Dickens Christmas celebration, which features carolers,

storytellers, and period-appropriate decorations and activities

2. Teenagers (13-18):
    ○ Learning about the social, economic, and political aspects of 19th-century life in Alabama through guided tours and interactive exhibits
    ○ Engaging with costumed interpreters to ask questions and gain a deeper understanding of the challenges and opportunities faced by early Alabamians
    ○ Participating in living history demonstrations, such as blacksmithing or printing, to appreciate the skills and techniques of the past
    ○ Exploring the museum's archives and research library to conduct historical research or work on school projects

3. Adults:
    ○ Gaining insights into the daily lives, customs, and values of 19th-century Alabamians through the museum's authentic exhibits and living history demonstrations
    ○ Attending lectures, workshops, and special events that delve into specific aspects of Alabama's history and culture
    ○ Participating in guided tours that provide a more in-depth look at the museum's collections and the stories behind the historic structures
    ○ Supporting the museum's mission of preserving and interpreting Alabama's past through volunteering, donating, or becoming a member

Amenities and accessibility:

- The museum offers restroom facilities and a small gift shop that sells books, souvenirs, and period-inspired items
- Some of the historic buildings have limited accessibility due to their original designs, but the museum strives to accommodate visitors with mobility issues as much as possible
- Guided tours and living history demonstrations are included with admission, providing a structured and informative experience for visitors
- The museum has a small parking lot, and additional street parking is available in the surrounding area

Special events and programs: Old Alabama Town hosts a variety of special events and programs throughout the year, including:

- The Dickens Christmas celebration, which recreates the atmosphere of a Victorian-era holiday season with carolers, decorations, and themed activities
- The Frontier Days event, which focuses on the early settlement period of Alabama and features living history demonstrations, music, and food
- The "Loom to Loom" textile workshop, which teaches participants about traditional spinning, weaving, and dyeing techniques
- The "Blacksmithing Basics" workshop, which introduces participants to the art and science of blacksmithing and allows them to create a small project to take home

Other important information for visiting families:

- The museum is closed on Mondays and major holidays, so it's important to plan accordingly
- Visitors should allow at least 1-2 hours to fully explore the

museum and participate in the various activities and demonstrations

- Comfortable walking shoes are recommended, as the museum covers several acres and features uneven surfaces and stairs in some areas
- Photography is permitted throughout the museum, but visitors should be respectful of the historic structures and artifacts
- The museum welcomes school groups and offers special programs and discounts for educators and students

Old Alabama Town is a must-visit destination for families interested in history, culture, and the unique heritage of Alabama. By providing an immersive and engaging experience that brings the past to life, the museum encourages visitors to appreciate the challenges and triumphs of earlier generations and to understand the forces that have shaped the state and its people. Whether you're a local resident or a visitor from out of town, Old Alabama Town offers a fascinating and educational journey through time that is sure to leave a lasting impression on visitors of all ages.

Montgomery Museum of Fine Arts

(Montgomery)

Address: 300 S Jackson St, Montgomery, AL 36104

Phone: (334) 240-4333

Hours: Tuesday-Saturday 10 AM - 5 PM, Sunday 12 PM - 5 PM (Closed Mondays)

Admission: Adults $10, Children (6-11) $5, Children under 6 free

The Montgomery Museum of Fine Arts is a fantastic destination for families looking to explore the world of art, spark their creativity, and engage in meaningful learning experiences. With its diverse collections, educational programs, and family-friendly amenities, the museum offers a welcoming and enriching environment for visitors of all ages and backgrounds.

Activities and attractions for different age groups:

1. Toddlers and young children (2-5):
    - Exploring the museum's interactive "ArtWorks" gallery, which features hands-on activities and multi-sensory experiences designed to introduce young children to the world of art
    - Participating in the museum's "Artful Tots" program, which offers age-appropriate art classes and storytimes for children aged 2-5 and their caregivers
    - Enjoying the museum's outdoor sculpture garden, which provides a safe and engaging space for young children to explore and play

2. Elementary school-aged children (6-12):
    - Discovering the museum's diverse art collections through guided tours and gallery activities that encourage critical thinking, creativity, and self-expression
    - Participating in the museum's "Saturday Studio" program, which offers in-depth art classes and workshops for children aged 6-12, covering a range of mediums and techniques
    - Exploring the museum's temporary exhibitions, which often feature interactive elements and family-friendly themes that capture children's imaginations and curiosity

3. Teenagers (13-18):
    - Engaging with the museum's collections and exhibitions through guided tours, audio guides, and self-directed exploration
    - Participating in the museum's teen programs, such as the "Teen Council" or "Summer Art Camp," which provide opportunities for skill-building, socialization, and creative expression
    - Attending special events, such as artist talks, film screenings, or performances, that connect the visual arts to other forms of creative expression and contemporary issues

4. Adults:
    - Appreciating the depth and breadth of the museum's collections, which span a wide range of cultures, time periods, and artistic styles
    - Attending lectures, workshops, and special events that provide deeper insights into the art world and the creative process

- ○ Participating in guided tours or using audio guides to gain a more comprehensive understanding of the artworks and their historical and cultural contexts
- ○ Supporting the museum's mission through membership, volunteering, or donating to help sustain its programs and exhibitions

Amenities and accessibility:

- The museum offers a gift shop that sells art-related books, souvenirs, and unique items inspired by the collections
- The museum has a small café that serves light refreshments and snacks
- All public spaces in the museum are wheelchair accessible, and wheelchairs are available for loan at the front desk
- The museum provides free parking in its adjacent lot, with designated spaces for visitors with disabilities
- Restrooms with changing tables are available on each floor of the museum
- The museum offers sensory-friendly resources, such as noise-canceling headphones and fidget toys, for visitors who may benefit from them

Special programs and events: The Montgomery Museum of Fine Arts offers a variety of special programs and events throughout the year, including:

- The "Jazz Jams" series, which features live jazz performances in the museum's outdoor sculpture garden
- The "Art in the Garden" event, which showcases the work of local artists and craftspeople in an outdoor festival setting

- The "Family Art Affair" program, which provides monthly art-making activities and performances for families with children of all ages
- The "Ekphrasis" series, which explores the connections between visual art and creative writing through readings, discussions, and workshops

Other important information for visiting families:

- The museum is closed on Mondays and major holidays, so it's important to plan accordingly
- Admission is free for museum members and children under 6, and discounted rates are available for students, seniors, and military personnel
- The museum offers a variety of membership options that provide benefits such as free admission, discounts on programs and events, and reciprocal privileges at other museums
- Photography is permitted in most areas of the museum, but visitors should refrain from using flash or tripods and respect any posted restrictions
- Large bags and backpacks must be checked at the front desk or stored in the museum's lockers

The Montgomery Museum of Fine Arts is a must-visit destination for families who want to explore the world of art, nurture their creativity, and engage in meaningful learning experiences. With its commitment to accessibility, education, and community engagement, the museum provides a welcoming and inclusive space where visitors of all ages and backgrounds can discover the transformative power of art. Whether you're a lifelong art lover or a curious newcomer, the Montgomery Museum of Fine Arts offers a wealth of opportunities to explore, learn, and be inspired by the beauty and diversity of human creativity.

Alabama Nature Center

(Millbrook)

Address: 3050 Lanark Rd, Millbrook, AL 36054

Phone: (334) 285-4550

Hours: Tuesday-Saturday 10 AM - 5 PM, Sunday 1 PM - 5 PM (Closed Mondays)

Admission: Adults $6, Children (3-12) $4, Children under 3 free

The Alabama Nature Center is a fantastic destination for families looking to connect with nature, explore the great outdoors, and engage in meaningful learning experiences. With its diverse habitats, interactive exhibits, and educational programs, the center offers a unique and enriching environment for visitors of all ages and backgrounds.

Activities and attractions for different age groups:

1. Toddlers and young children (2-5):
    - Exploring the center's "Discovery Room," which features hands-on activities, nature-themed play areas, and live animal displays designed to introduce young children to the wonders of the natural world
    - Participating in the center's "Nature Tykes" program, which offers age-appropriate nature walks, stories, and crafts for children aged 2-5 and their caregivers
    - Enjoying the center's outdoor play areas, which provide safe and engaging spaces for young

children to explore and connect with nature

2. Elementary school-aged children (6-12):
    ◦ Hiking the center's trails and participating in guided nature walks, which offer opportunities to observe and learn about the diverse plants, animals, and ecosystems of Alabama
    ◦ Engaging in the center's "Junior Naturalist" program, which provides hands-on activities, experiments, and challenges that teach children about ecology, conservation, and environmental stewardship
    ◦ Exploring the center's interactive exhibits, which showcase the unique habitats, wildlife, and natural resources of the region

3. Teenagers (13-18):
    ◦ Participating in the center's "Teen Volunteer" program, which offers opportunities to assist with trail maintenance, animal care, and educational programs while gaining valuable leadership and naturalist skills
    ◦ Attending the center's "Nature Photography" workshops, which provide instruction and guidance on capturing the beauty and diversity of the natural world through digital photography
    ◦ Joining the center's "Outdoor Adventure" programs, which offer challenges such as orienteering, archery, and survival skills that promote self-reliance, teamwork, and environmental awareness

4. Adults:
    ◦ Hiking the center's trails and enjoying the peaceful beauty of the natural surroundings

- Attending the center's workshops, lectures, and special events, which cover topics such as native plant gardening, birdwatching, and environmental conservation
- Volunteering with the center's various programs and initiatives, such as habitat restoration projects, citizen science efforts, and community outreach events
- Supporting the center's mission through membership, donations, or advocacy efforts that help protect and preserve Alabama's natural heritage

Amenities and accessibility:

- The center offers a visitor center with restrooms, a gift shop, and a small exhibit area
- Picnic tables and benches are available throughout the center's grounds, providing spots for families to rest, relax, and enjoy a packed lunch
- The center's trails vary in difficulty and accessibility, with some trails being wheelchair and stroller-friendly while others are more rugged and challenging
- The center provides ample parking, with designated spaces for visitors with disabilities
- The center's indoor facilities are wheelchair accessible, and the staff is available to assist visitors with special needs or accommodations

Special programs and events: The Alabama Nature Center offers a variety of special programs and events throughout the year, including:

- The "Maple Syrup Making" program, which demonstrates the traditional process of harvesting and boiling maple sap to create pure maple syrup
- The "Monarch Butterfly Festival," which celebrates the annual migration of monarch butterflies and features tagged butterfly releases, educational exhibits, and family-friendly activities
- The "Audubon Bird Count" events, which engage citizen scientists in collecting data on bird populations and migrations in the region
- The "Yoga in Nature" series, which combines the physical and mental benefits of yoga with the peaceful and restorative power of the natural world

Other important information for visiting families:

- The center is closed on Mondays and major holidays, so it's essential to plan accordingly
- Admission fees support the center's programs, facilities, and conservation efforts, and discounted rates are available for members, students, and seniors
- The center offers a variety of membership options that provide benefits such as free admission, discounts on programs and events, and special member-only opportunities
- Visitors should come prepared with appropriate clothing, footwear, sun protection, insect repellent, and water, especially during the warmer months
- The center promotes a "leave no trace" ethic, encouraging visitors to pack out their trash, stay on designated trails, and respect the natural environment and wildlife

The Alabama Nature Center is a must-visit destination for families who want to connect with the natural world, explore the rich biodiversity of Alabama, and engage in meaningful learning experiences. With its commitment to environmental education, conservation, and community engagement, the center provides a welcoming and inspiring space where visitors of all ages and backgrounds can discover the wonders and importance of the natural world. Whether you're a seasoned naturalist or a curious newcomer, the Alabama Nature Center offers a wealth of opportunities to explore, learn, and be inspired by the beauty and complexity of the natural systems that sustain us all.

Playhouse Theatre

(Montgomery)

Address: 4623 Mobile Hwy, Montgomery, AL 36108

Phone: (334) 271-5353

Hours: Show times and schedules vary

Admission: Ticket prices vary based on show and seating

The Playhouse Theatre is a wonderful destination for families seeking to introduce their children to the enchanting world of live theatre. With its commitment to producing high-quality, family-friendly shows and providing educational opportunities, the theatre offers a unique and enriching experience for young audiences and their families.

Activities and attractions for different age groups:

1. Toddlers and preschoolers (2-5):
    - Attending specially designed "Theatre for the Very Young" performances, which feature shorter run times, interactive elements, and age-appropriate themes and content
    - Participating in "Mommy and Me" or "Daddy and Me" theatre classes, which provide a fun and engaging introduction to drama and storytelling for young children and their caregivers
    - Enjoying pre-show activities, such as crafts, games, and story times, that help prepare young children for the theatre experience
2. Elementary school-aged children (6-12):

- ○ Watching main stage productions of classic and contemporary children's stories, which feature colorful costumes, imaginative sets, and talented performers
- ○ Attending "Behind the Scenes" workshops, which offer a glimpse into the world of theatre production, including set design, costume creation, and special effects
- ○ Participating in summer theatre camps and after-school drama classes, which provide opportunities for skill-building, creative expression, and social interaction

3. Teenagers (13-18):
- ○ Enjoying family-friendly musicals, comedies, and dramas that tackle relevant themes and issues for adolescent audiences
- ○ Attending "Teen Night" performances, which feature post-show discussions and activities designed to engage and inspire teenage theatre-goers
- ○ Participating in advanced acting classes, technical theatre workshops, and performance opportunities through the theatre's education program

4. Adults:
- ○ Accompanying their children to live performances and sharing in the joy and wonder of the theatre experience
- ○ Attending "Parent and Child" workshops, which provide opportunities for families to bond and learn together through creative drama activities
- ○ Supporting the theatre's mission and programs

through volunteering, donations, or membership in the theatre's "Friends and Family" organization

Amenities and accessibility:

- The theatre offers concessions, including snacks and beverages, for purchase before the show and during intermission
- Restrooms and changing tables are available in the theatre's lobby
- The theatre is wheelchair accessible, with designated seating areas and assistance provided by theatre staff
- Assistive listening devices and sensory-friendly performances are available for select shows, accommodating children with varying needs and sensitivities
- The theatre provides nearby parking, with some spaces designated for visitors with disabilities

Special programs and events: The Playhouse Theatre offers a variety of special programs and events throughout the year, including:

- "Page to Stage" book club, which brings popular children's books to life through dramatic readings, discussions, and related activities
- "Family Fun Days," which feature interactive performances, workshops, and activities centered around a specific theme or story
- "Sensory-Friendly Saturdays," which provide a welcoming and accommodating theatre experience for children with sensory processing disorders or other special needs
- "Holiday Spectaculars," which showcase festive and beloved stories and traditions during the winter holiday season

Other important information for visiting families:

- Show times and ticket prices vary depending on the production and seating section, so it's essential to check the theatre's website or box office for the most up-to-date information
- Advance ticket purchases are recommended, especially for popular shows or peak performance times
- The theatre offers group discounts and school field trip packages, making it an ideal destination for birthday parties, scouting troops, or educational outings
- Booster seats are available for young children to ensure good visibility of the stage
- The theatre maintains a "Quiet Room" in the lobby, where parents can take children who need a break from the performance without missing the show entirely

The Playhouse Theatre is a must-visit destination for families who want to share the joy, creativity, and learning experiences that live theatre provides. By offering a diverse range of productions, educational programs, and accessibility features, the theatre ensures that children of all ages and backgrounds can engage with the transformative power of storytelling and performance. Whether you're a regular theatre-goer or a first-time visitor, the Playhouse Theatre promises a magical and memorable experience that will inspire a lifelong love of the performing arts.

MONTGOMERY
Biscuits

Montgomery Biscuits Baseball

(Montgomery)

Address: 1000 Ted Davidson Way, Montgomery, AL 36109

Phone: (334) 323-2255

Hours: Game schedules and times vary

Admission: Ticket prices vary based on seating

A Montgomery Biscuits baseball game is a fantastic way for families to spend quality time together while enjoying the excitement of America's pastime. With its welcoming atmosphere, engaging promotions, and family-friendly amenities, Riverwalk Stadium offers a memorable experience for fans of all ages.

Activities and attractions for different age groups:

1. Toddlers and young children (2-5):
    - Enjoying the lively atmosphere, music, and cheering crowds at the stadium
    - Participating in between-inning games and activities, such as the "Toddler Trot" or "Dance Cam"
    - Visiting the team mascot, "Big Mo," for photos and high-fives
    - Playing in the stadium's designated children's area, which features playground equipment and inflatables
2. Elementary school-aged children (6-12):
    - Learning about the rules and strategies of baseball by watching the game and asking questions

- Participating in "Kids Run the Bases" events after select games, where children can run the bases and meet players
- Collecting player autographs and trading baseball cards with other young fans
- Enjoying special kid-focused promotions, such as "Kids Eat Free" nights or "Scout Sleepovers" at the stadium

3. Teenagers (13-18):
    - Appreciating the skill and athleticism of the Minor League players and aspiring to excel in their own sports or interests
    - Socializing with friends and family in the stadium's vibrant and welcoming atmosphere
    - Participating in interactive games and contests, such as trivia challenges or social media photo competitions
    - Learning about career opportunities in sports, including athletic training, sports journalism, and event management

4. Adults:
    - Bonding with their children over a shared love of baseball and creating lasting family memories
    - Enjoying the affordable entertainment and family-friendly atmosphere of Minor League Baseball
    - Savoring classic ballpark fare and local specialties from the stadium's concession stands and food trucks
    - Relaxing and unwinding in the stadium's scenic setting along the Alabama River

Amenities and accessibility:

- The stadium offers a variety of concession stands and food options, including vegetarian and gluten-free choices
- Restrooms and changing tables are located throughout the stadium for family convenience
- The stadium is wheelchair accessible, with designated seating areas and assistance provided by guest services staff
- Assisted listening devices are available for guests with hearing impairments
- The stadium provides nearby parking, with some spaces designated for visitors with disabilities

Special programs and events: The Montgomery Biscuits offer a variety of special programs and events throughout the season, including:

- "Bark in the Park" nights, where fans can bring their furry friends to the game and enjoy pet-friendly activities and promotions
- "Military Appreciation" nights, which honor active-duty service members, veterans, and their families with special recognition and discounts
- "Thirsty Thursday" promotions, featuring discounted beverages and live music for adult fans
- "Fireworks Spectaculars," which light up the sky after select games and create a dazzling display for fans of all ages

Other important information for visiting families:

- Game times and ticket prices vary depending on the day of the week and the opposing team, so it's essential to check the team's website or box office for the most up-to-date information
- Advance ticket purchases are recommended, especially for

popular games or promotional events

- The stadium offers group discounts and birthday party packages, making it an ideal destination for celebrations or team outings
- Outside food and beverages are not permitted in the stadium, but exceptions may be made for guests with special dietary needs or infants
- The team maintains a "Guest Assistance" booth in the stadium, where fans can seek help, report concerns, or receive first aid if needed

A Montgomery Biscuits baseball game is a must-do experience for families looking to create lasting memories, celebrate America's pastime, and enjoy an affordable and engaging outing together. With its commitment to providing a welcoming and entertaining atmosphere for fans of all ages, Riverwalk Stadium ensures that every visit to a Biscuits game is a home run for family fun. Whether you're a die-hard baseball fan or simply looking for a unique and exciting way to spend quality time together, a Montgomery Biscuits game promises an unforgettable experience that will have your family cheering for more.

#EASTCHASE

Eastchase Shopping Center

(Montgomery)

Address: 7061 EastChase Pkwy, Montgomery, AL 36117

Phone: (334) 279-6046

Hours: Monday-Saturday 10 AM - 9 PM, Sunday 12 PM - 6 PM

Admission: Free (individual store prices may vary)

Eastchase Shopping Center is a fantastic destination for families looking to enjoy a day of shopping, dining, and entertainment in a welcoming and vibrant atmosphere. With its diverse mix of retailers, family-friendly amenities, and special events, the center offers something for everyone, making it a popular choice for Montgomery families.

Activities and attractions for different age groups:

1. Toddlers and young children (2-5):
    - Enjoying the center's outdoor play area, which features soft surfaces, climbing structures, and interactive elements designed for young children
    - Riding the colorful carousel, a classic attraction that delights children of all ages
    - Participating in seasonal events and activities, such as holiday crafts, face painting, or character meet-and-greets
2. Elementary school-aged children (6-12):
    - Exploring the center's various stores and discovering new interests, such as books, toys, or hobbies

- Enjoying a treat or snack from one of the center's many eateries or sweet shops
- Taking part in special events and promotions, such as scavenger hunts, contests, or live performances

3. Teenagers (13-18):
    - Shopping for the latest fashion trends and accessories at popular clothing retailers
    - Socializing with friends and family in the center's open-air common areas or outdoor seating areas
    - Attending special events and activities geared towards teens, such as live music performances or movie screenings

4. Adults:
    - Browsing the wide selection of retailers and finding great deals on clothing, home goods, and gifts
    - Enjoying a meal or refreshing beverage at one of the center's many dining options, from quick bites to sit-down restaurants
    - Relaxing in the center's inviting outdoor spaces, which feature comfortable seating, landscaping, and water features
    - Taking advantage of special sales, promotions, or events offered by individual stores or the center as a whole

Amenities and accessibility:

- The center offers ample parking, with some spaces designated for visitors with disabilities
- Restrooms and changing tables are located throughout the center for family convenience

- The center is wheelchair accessible, with wide, level walkways and automatic doors at most store entrances
- Many stores offer amenities such as gift wrapping, personal shopping assistance, or curbside pickup for added convenience
- The center provides free Wi-Fi in common areas, allowing visitors to stay connected while shopping or dining

Special programs and events: Eastchase Shopping Center hosts a variety of special programs and events throughout the year, including:

- "Kids Club" events, which feature family-friendly activities, crafts, and entertainment on select weekends
- "Girls' Night Out" promotions, offering exclusive discounts, giveaways, and pampering experiences for female shoppers
- "Sip & Shop" events, which combine shopping with wine tastings or cocktail samplings at participating stores and restaurants
- Seasonal celebrations, such as holiday tree lightings, Easter egg hunts, or summer concert series

Other important information for visiting families:

- Store hours may vary, so it's essential to check individual store listings or the center's website for the most up-to-date information
- Some stores or restaurants may have age restrictions or policies regarding unaccompanied minors, so it's important to be aware of these guidelines
- The center offers gift cards, which can be purchased at the information desk or online and used at most stores and

restaurants

- Strollers are permitted throughout the center, but some stores may have policies regarding strollers during busy periods or in certain areas
- The center maintains a "Lost and Found" service at the information desk, where visitors can report or claim lost items

Eastchase Shopping Center is a must-visit destination for Montgomery families seeking a one-stop shop for retail therapy, dining delights, and family-friendly fun. With its commitment to providing a welcoming and engaging atmosphere for visitors of all ages, the center ensures that every shopping trip is a memorable experience filled with discovery, relaxation, and quality time together. Whether you're looking to update your wardrobe, find the perfect gift, or simply enjoy a day out with loved ones, Eastchase Shopping Center promises a rewarding and enjoyable experience that will keep your family coming back for more.

Urban Air Trampoline Park

(Montgomery)

Address: 8030 Vaughn Rd, Montgomery, AL 36116

Phone: (334) 356-9990

Hours: Monday-Thursday 3 PM - 8 PM, Friday 3 PM - 10 PM, Saturday 10 AM - 10 PM, Sunday 12 PM - 8 PM

Admission: Prices vary based on activity and time, but typically around $15-$20 for 1-hour jump pass

Urban Air Trampoline Park is an exciting destination for families seeking a thrilling and active indoor experience. With its wide variety of attractions, safety features, and special events, the park offers a fun-filled outing that encourages physical activity, social interaction, and unforgettable memories.

Activities and attractions for different age groups:

1. Toddlers and young children (2-5):
    ◦ Exploring the dedicated toddler area, which features smaller trampolines, foam pits, and soft play structures designed for safe and age-appropriate play
    ◦ Participating in "Jumperoo" sessions, special jump times reserved for children 5 and under and their caregivers
    ◦ Enjoying the park's colorful and imaginative décor, which creates a whimsical and inviting atmosphere for young visitors
2. Elementary school-aged children (6-12):

- Bouncing and flipping on the main trampoline area, which offers over 10,000 square feet of interconnected trampolines
- Playing trampoline dodgeball, basketball, or participating in the trampoline-infused obstacle course
- Challenging themselves on the park's warrior course or climbing walls, which promote strength, agility, and problem-solving skills
- Attending "Kid Jump" sessions, special jump times reserved for children 12 and under

3. Teenagers (13-18):
   - Mastering advanced flips, tricks, and techniques on the main trampoline area or in the dedicated tumbling lanes
   - Competing with friends in trampoline dodgeball tournaments or slam dunk contests
   - Participating in "Teen Night" events, which feature extended park hours, live DJ music, and special giveaways for teenage jumpers
   - Challenging themselves on the park's more advanced attractions, such as the Battle Beam or the Drop Zone

4. Adults:
   - Joining their children on the trampolines and enjoying a fun and active family outing together
   - Participating in "Adult Night" events, which offer a grown-up jumping experience with extended park hours and special activities
   - Booking the park for private events, such as corporate team-building sessions or fitness classes
   - Cheering on their children from the observation

deck and capturing memorable photos and videos of their jumping adventures

Safety and accessibility: Urban Air Trampoline Park prioritizes safety and strives to create an inclusive environment for all guests. The following measures are in place:

- All jumpers must complete a safety waiver and watch a brief safety video before participating
- The park employs trained staff to monitor jumping areas and ensure that guests follow safety guidelines
- Jumpers are required to wear special grip socks, which are provided by the park, to reduce the risk of slips and falls
- The park features padded walls, foam pits, and other safety elements to minimize the risk of injury
- The park is wheelchair accessible, with ramps and wide pathways for easy navigation

Special programs and events: Urban Air Trampoline Park offers a variety of special programs and events throughout the year, including:

- "Sensory Friendly Jumps," which provide a low-stimulation environment for children with sensory processing disorders or special needs
- "Homeschool Jumps," which offer discounted admission and educational activities for homeschooled students and their families
- "Toddler Time," special jump sessions designed for children 5 and under and their caregivers
- Birthday party packages, which include private party rooms, dedicated party hosts, and customizable options for food and activities

Other important information for visiting families:

- Socks are required for all jumpers and can be purchased at the park if needed
- Jumpers should wear comfortable, athletic clothing and remove all jewelry and sharp objects before jumping
- Outside food and drinks are not permitted in the park, but guests may bring water bottles or purchase refreshments from the park's concession stand
- Lockers are available for rent to store personal belongings while jumping
- The park offers special discounts and promotions throughout the year, so it's a good idea to check their website or social media for the latest offers

Urban Air Trampoline Park is a must-visit destination for Montgomery families seeking a fun, active, and memorable indoor experience. With its impressive array of attractions, commitment to safety and inclusivity, and exciting special events, the park provides an unforgettable outing that promotes physical fitness, social interaction, and pure joy. Whether you're celebrating a birthday, enjoying a family day out, or simply looking to bounce away some energy, Urban Air Trampoline Park guarantees an exhilarating adventure that will leave you and your loved ones smiling from ear to ear.

Alabama Safari Park

(Hope Hull)

Address: 1856 Alamuchee Ridge Rd, Hope Hull, AL 36043

Phone: (334) 288-2105

Hours: Daily from 9 AM to 5 PM

Admission: Adults $19.95, Children (3-12) $14.95, Children under 3 free

The Alabama Safari Park is a fantastic destination for families looking to embark on an exciting and educational wildlife adventure. With its unique drive-through and walk-through experiences, the park offers visitors of all ages the chance to observe and interact with a diverse array of exotic animals in a safe and engaging environment.

Activities and attractions for different age groups:

1. Toddlers and young children (2-5):
     - Observing the animals from the safety and comfort of the family vehicle during the drive-through safari
     - Feeding the friendly animals in the walk-through area, such as goats and sheep, under adult supervision
     - Enjoying the park's playgrounds and picnic areas, which provide space for outdoor play and relaxation
2. Elementary school-aged children (6-12):
     - Learning about the animals' habitats, behaviors, and conservation status through guided tours and

educational displays

- Participating in the park's "Junior Zookeeper" program, which offers behind-the-scenes experiences and hands-on animal encounters
- Exploring the walk-through area and discovering the unique characteristics of animals like kangaroos, lemurs, and parakeets

3. Teenagers (13-18):

- Capturing amazing photos and videos of the animals in their natural habitats during the drive-through safari
- Assisting younger siblings in feeding and interacting with animals in the walk-through area
- Participating in the park's educational programs or volunteer opportunities, which can provide valuable experience for those interested in animal-related careers

4. Adults:

- Driving the family vehicle through the safari park and enjoying the rare opportunity to observe exotic animals up close
- Learning about animal conservation and the importance of preserving biodiversity through guided tours and educational exhibits
- Relaxing in the park's scenic picnic areas or exploring the gift shop for unique souvenirs and animal-themed merchandise

Safety and accessibility: The Alabama Safari Park prioritizes the safety of both visitors and animals. The following measures are in place:

- Visitors must remain in their vehicles at all times during the drive-through safari, with windows and doors closed when instructed

- The park provides clear guidelines and instructions for feeding and interacting with animals in the walk-through area
- The park is wheelchair accessible, with paved pathways in the walk-through area and the ability to drive through the safari in personal vehicles
- Hand-washing stations and restrooms are available throughout the park to promote hygiene and cleanliness

Special programs and events: The Alabama Safari Park offers a variety of special programs and events throughout the year, including:

- "Keeper Talks," which provide visitors with insights into animal care, behavior, and conservation efforts from the park's expert zookeepers
- "Animal Encounters," which allow visitors to get up close and personal with select animals under the guidance of trained staff
- "Safari Camp," a summer program that offers children ages 6-12 the opportunity to learn about animals, conservation, and zoo careers through hands-on activities and behind-the-scenes experiences
- Special holiday events, such as "Boo at the Zoo" for Halloween and "Holiday Lights" during the winter season

Other important information for visiting families:

- The park is open year-round, with extended hours during peak summer months
- Visitors should allow at least 1-2 hours to fully experience

both the drive-through safari and walk-through areas
- Food and drinks are available for purchase at the park's concession stands, and picnic areas are provided for those who wish to bring their own meals
- The park offers a variety of ticket options, including discounted rates for seniors, military personnel, and groups
- Photography is encouraged, but visitors should refrain from using flash or disturbing the animals in any way

The Alabama Safari Park is a must-visit destination for families seeking a unique and memorable wildlife experience. By offering a combination of drive-through and walk-through animal encounters, educational programs, and family-friendly amenities, the park provides an immersive and engaging adventure that fosters a deeper appreciation for the natural world and the incredible creatures that inhabit it. Whether you're a local resident or a visitor to the Montgomery area, the Alabama Safari Park promises an unforgettable journey through the wild side of Alabama.

WELCOME TO
RIVERFRONT
MONTGOMERY ALABAMA

Montgomery Riverfront Park

(Montgomery)

Address: 285 Water St, Montgomery, AL 36104

Phone: (334) 625-2333

Hours: Park grounds open daily from 6 AM to 10 PM

Admission: Free

Montgomery Riverfront Park is a delightful destination for families looking to enjoy outdoor recreation, scenic beauty, and quality time together in the heart of the city. With its diverse amenities, engaging activities, and picturesque setting along the Alabama River, the park offers a refreshing and enjoyable experience for visitors of all ages.

Activities and attractions for different age groups:

1. Toddlers and young children (2-5):
    - Playing in the splash pad area, which features age-appropriate water jets, sprayers, and interactive elements designed for safe and fun aquatic play
    - Exploring the park's playground, which offers climbing structures, swings, and other equipment suitable for young children
    - Enjoying picnics or snack time with family in the park's lush green spaces or covered pavilion
2. Elementary school-aged children (6-12):
    - Participating in organized games and activities on the park's open lawn areas, such as frisbee, tag, or kite-flying
    - Riding bikes, scooters, or rollerblades along the

park's paved trails or riverwalk
- Attending family-friendly events and festivals held at the park throughout the year, such as outdoor concerts or holiday celebrations

3. Teenagers (13-18):
- Enjoying the scenic views and fresh air while walking, jogging, or biking along the riverwalk
- Socializing with friends and family in the park's picturesque settings, such as the amphitheater or riverfront promenade
- Participating in community events or volunteer opportunities, such as river clean-up days or park beautification projects

4. Adults:
- Strolling hand-in-hand along the riverwalk, enjoying the romantic ambiance and stunning views of the Alabama River and city skyline
- Relaxing on a bench or picnic blanket, reading a book, or simply taking in the peaceful surroundings
- Attending outdoor fitness classes, such as yoga or tai chi, offered in the park's scenic locations
- Participating in guided nature walks or historical tours that showcase the park's rich cultural heritage and ecological significance

Amenities and accessibility:

- The park offers ample seating options, including benches, picnic tables, and an amphitheater-style seating area
- Restrooms and drinking fountains are available throughout the park for visitor convenience
- The park is wheelchair accessible, with paved paths, ramps,

and designated parking spaces for visitors with disabilities
- Trash and recycling receptacles are located throughout the park to encourage cleanliness and environmental stewardship
- The park provides free Wi-Fi in select areas, allowing visitors to stay connected while enjoying the outdoors

Special events and programs: Montgomery Riverfront Park hosts a variety of special events and programs throughout the year, including:

- "Sunday at the Park" concert series, featuring live musical performances from local and regional artists
- "Movies in the Park" events, which offer free outdoor screenings of family-friendly films under the stars
- "Riverfront Market," a seasonal farmers market showcasing locally-grown produce, artisanal goods, and food vendors
- Annual festivals and celebrations, such as the "Juneteenth Cultural Arts Festival" and the "Christmas on the River" holiday extravaganza

Other important information for visiting families:

- The park is open daily from sunrise to sunset, with extended hours for special events and programs
- Parking is available in nearby garages and lots, with some metered street parking also available
- The park is patrolled by local law enforcement and park rangers to ensure visitor safety and security
- Visitors are encouraged to follow park rules and guidelines, such as properly disposing of waste, respecting wildlife, and sharing the space with other park users
- In case of inclement weather or emergency situations,

visitors should follow the instructions of park staff or local authorities

Montgomery Riverfront Park is a must-visit destination for families seeking a tranquil escape, outdoor recreation, and quality time together in the heart of the city. By offering a wide range of amenities, activities, and events that cater to diverse interests and age groups, the park provides a welcoming and inclusive space that encourages healthy living, community engagement, and appreciation for the natural beauty of the Alabama River. Whether you're a Montgomery resident or a visitor exploring the city's attractions, Montgomery Riverfront Park promises a delightful and memorable experience that will leave you feeling refreshed, inspired, and connected to the vibrant pulse of this historic Southern city.

THE ORCHARD
oudler Valley

Children's Hand-On Museum

(Huntsville)

Address: 219 Parkway Place NW, Huntsville, AL 35806

Phone: (256) 837-0201

Hours: Tuesday-Saturday 9 AM - 4 PM, Sunday 1 PM - 4 PM (Closed Mondays) Admission: Adults $10, Children (2-17) $10, Children under 2 free

The Children's Hand-On Museum in Huntsville is a fantastic destination for families with young children, offering a wide range of interactive exhibits, educational programs, and hands-on activities that promote learning through play. With its focus on creativity, exploration, and discovery, the museum provides a stimulating and engaging environment that encourages children to learn while having fun.

Activities and attractions for different age groups:

1. Toddlers and preschoolers (2-5):
     - Exploring the "Itty Bitty City" exhibit, which features a miniature town designed for imaginative play and role-playing
     - Engaging with sensory-rich activities in the "Tactile & Texture" area, which promotes fine motor skills and sensory development
     - Enjoying the "Little Sprouts" garden-themed play area, which encourages nature exploration and imaginative play
2. Elementary school-aged children (6-12):
     - Discovering the principles of science, technology,

engineering, and math (STEM) through hands-on exhibits like the "Invention Convention" and "Science Lab"
    ◦ Expressing their creativity in the "Art Studio," which offers a variety of materials and projects for artistic exploration
    ◦ Engaging in cooperative play and problem-solving in the "Construction Zone," which features building materials and challenges
3. Teenagers and adults:
    ◦ Accompanying younger children and facilitating their learning experiences through guided exploration and discussion
    ◦ Participating in family-oriented workshops, special events, or educational programs offered by the museum
    ◦ Discovering the joy of learning alongside their children and fostering a shared love for knowledge and discovery

Amenities and accessibility:

- The museum offers a small gift shop with educational toys, books, and souvenirs
- Restrooms and changing tables are available for family convenience
- The museum is wheelchair accessible, with ramps, elevators, and wide pathways for easy navigation
- Quiet spaces and sensory-friendly kits are available for children who may become overwhelmed by stimulating environments
- The museum provides lockers for storing personal belongings during your visit

Educational programs and special events: The Children's Hand-On Museum offers a variety of educational programs and special events throughout the year, including:

- "Little Learners" classes, which provide structured learning experiences for preschoolers and their caregivers
- "Homeschool Hangouts," which offer hands-on learning opportunities and socialization for homeschooled children
- "Super Saturday" events, featuring special themes, guest presenters, and extended hours for family fun and learning
- Summer camps and workshops, which provide in-depth exploration of specific topics or themes for various age groups

Membership and support: The museum offers membership options for families and individuals, which provide benefits such as:

- Unlimited admission to the museum for a year
- Discounts on educational programs, camps, and special events
- Reciprocal admission to other participating children's museums across the country
- Invitations to member-only events and previews
- Supporting the museum's mission and educational initiatives through financial contributions

Tips for visiting:

- Plan to spend at least 2-3 hours exploring the museum's exhibits and activities
- Encourage your children to take their time, ask questions, and engage with the exhibits in their own way
- Bring a lunch or snack to enjoy in the museum's designated

eating areas, as outside food is not permitted in the exhibit spaces

- Consider visiting during off-peak hours (weekday afternoons or Sunday) for a more relaxed experience
- Check the museum's website or social media pages for information on current exhibits, programs, and special events

The Children's Hand-On Museum in Huntsville is a must-visit destination for families seeking a fun, educational, and interactive experience that nurtures a love for learning and discovery. By providing a wide range of hands-on exhibits, programs, and amenities designed specifically for young learners, the museum creates a welcoming and inclusive environment that encourages children to explore, create, and grow. Whether you're a local family or visiting from out of town, the Children's Hand-On Museum promises a memorable and enriching experience that will spark your child's imagination and curiosity.

Bamahenge

(Weedon Field)

Address: 1585 County Rd 15, Weedon Field, AL 36679

Phone: N/A

Hours: Open 24/7

Admission: Free

Bamahenge is a one-of-a-kind roadside attraction that offers families a unique and memorable experience while exploring the rural countryside of Alabama. Although it may not provide a full day of activities, this whimsical art installation is sure to capture the imagination of visitors of all ages and spark conversations about history, art, and sustainability.

Attractions and talking points for different age groups:

1. Young children (2-8):
    - Marveling at the giant, upright vehicles and discussing their colors, shapes, and sizes
    - Playing "I Spy" to identify different types of vehicles and farm equipment used in the installation
    - Encouraging imaginative play and storytelling inspired by the unusual arrangement of the vehicles
2. Older children and teenagers (9-18):
    - Learning about the history and significance of the original Stonehenge monument and comparing it to Bamahenge

- Discussing the artistic process and the role of recycled materials in creating public art installations
- Exploring the themes of creativity, sustainability, and repurposing everyday objects for new purposes

3. Adults:
- Appreciating the whimsical nature of the art installation and its unique take on a historical monument
- Discussing the artist's intentions and the social commentary behind the use of vehicles and farm equipment
- Reflecting on the juxtaposition of ancient history and modern consumer culture represented by the installation

Photo opportunities and social media: Bamahenge provides an excellent backdrop for unique and memorable photos. Encourage your family to:

- Take selfies or group photos in front of the installation, using the vehicles as a quirky and eye-catching background
- Experiment with different angles and perspectives to capture the scale and arrangement of the vehicles
- Share photos on social media platforms, tagging the location and using relevant hashtags to share your experience with others

Educational opportunities: While visiting Bamahenge, take the opportunity to educate your family about:

- The history and significance of the original Stonehenge

monument, its construction, and the theories surrounding its purpose
- The role of public art in communities and how it can spark conversations, inspire creativity, and bring people together
- The importance of recycling, repurposing, and sustainable practices in art and everyday life

Nearby attractions and amenities:

- Bamahenge is located in a rural area, so there are limited amenities in the immediate vicinity
- The town of Enterprise, located approximately 30 miles away, offers a variety of dining, shopping, and lodging options
- Other nearby attractions include the Boll Weevil Monument in Enterprise and the Dothan Area Botanical Gardens, both within an hour's drive

Tips for visiting:

- Bamahenge is open 24/7 and is free to visit, making it a flexible and budget-friendly stop on your family road trip
- The installation is located on the side of a rural road, so be cautious of traffic when parking and exploring the site
- Bring water, snacks, and sun protection, as there are no amenities or shade available at the installation
- Be respectful of the art installation and the surrounding private property, and follow any posted rules or guidelines

Bamahenge may not be a typical family destination, but it offers a unique opportunity to experience a one-of-a-kind art installation that combines history, creativity, and sustainability. By engaging your family in conversations about the artwork, its significance, and the broader themes it represents, you can transform a quick roadside stop into a memorable and educational experience. So, the next time you're driving through southeast Alabama, be sure to make a detour to Weedon Field and discover the quirky charm of Bamahenge for yourself.

Tannehill Ironworks Historical State Park

(McCalla)

Address: 12632 Confederate Pkwy, McCalla, AL 35111

Phone: (205) 477-5711

Hours: Park grounds open daily from 8 AM to Sunset

Admission: Adults $5, Children (6-11) $3, Children under 6 free

Tannehill Ironworks Historical State Park is a fascinating destination that offers families a unique blend of history, education, and outdoor recreation. With its well-preserved historical structures, engaging living history demonstrations, and beautiful natural setting, the park provides an immersive and memorable experience for visitors of all ages.

Activities and attractions for different age groups:

1. Young children (2-8):
    - Exploring the park's historical buildings and structures, such as the furnaces and cabins
    - Participating in hands-on activities and crafts related to 19th-century life and iron production
    - Enjoying the park's playgrounds and picnic areas for outdoor play and family time
2. Older children and teenagers (9-18):
    - Learning about the iron production process and its significance in Alabama's history through guided tours and living history demonstrations
    - Participating in educational programs and

workshops focused on 19th-century skills and trades
- ◦ Hiking the park's trails to explore the natural beauty of the area and spot local wildlife
3. Adults:
    - ◦ Gaining a deeper understanding of Alabama's industrial heritage and the lives of the people who worked in the ironworks
    - ◦ Photographing the park's historic structures and scenic landscapes
    - ◦ Participating in special events, such as the annual "Tannehill Trade Days" or the "Dulcimer Festival"
    - ◦ Enjoying outdoor recreational activities, such as hiking, fishing, or picnicking

Amenities and accessibility:

- The park offers picnic areas with tables and grills for family gatherings and outdoor meals
- Restrooms and drinking fountains are located throughout the park for visitor convenience
- The park's visitor center and some historical buildings are wheelchair accessible
- Camping facilities are available, including RV sites with hookups and primitive tent sites
- The park has a country store that sells snacks, drinks, and souvenirs

Educational programs and living history demonstrations: Tannehill Ironworks Historical State Park offers a variety of educational programs and living history demonstrations throughout the year, including:

- Guided tours of the ironworks and historical buildings, led by knowledgeable park staff or volunteers
- Living history demonstrations showcasing 19th-century skills and trades, such as blacksmithing, spinning, and weaving
- Educational workshops and hands-on activities focused on topics like archaeology, natural history, and pioneer life
- Special events and festivals that celebrate the park's history and cultural heritage

Nearby attractions and accommodations:

- The park is located near the cities of Bessemer and Birmingham, which offer a variety of dining, shopping, and lodging options
- Other nearby attractions include the Alabama Mining Museum, the Birmingham Zoo, and the Barber Vintage Motorsports Museum
- For those interested in extending their stay, the park offers camping facilities, as well as cabins and cottages for rent

Tips for visiting:

- Check the park's website or social media pages for information on current events, programs, and operating hours
- Wear comfortable walking shoes and bring water, sunscreen, and insect repellent for outdoor exploration
- Consider bringing a picnic lunch to enjoy in the park's scenic picnic areas
- Be respectful of the park's historical structures and artifacts, and follow any posted rules or guidelines
- Engage with the park's knowledgeable staff and volunteers

to learn more about the site's history and significance

Tannehill Ironworks Historical State Park is a must-visit destination for families interested in exploring Alabama's rich industrial heritage and enjoying the great outdoors. By providing a unique combination of historical education, living history demonstrations, and recreational activities, the park offers a well-rounded and engaging experience that appeals to visitors of all ages. Whether you're a history buff, an outdoor enthusiast, or simply looking for a unique and meaningful family outing, Tannehill Ironworks Historical State Park is sure to leave a lasting impression and provide valuable insights into Alabama's past and present.

USS Alabama Battleship Memorial Park

(Mobile)

Address: 2703 Battleship Pkwy, Mobile, AL 36602

Phone: (251) 433-2703

Hours: Daily from 8 AM to 6 PM

Admission: Adults $16, Children (6-12) $6, Children under 6 free

The USS Alabama Battleship Memorial Park is an incredible destination that offers families a unique blend of history, adventure, and outdoor recreation. With its awe-inspiring battleship, engaging exhibits, and beautiful park setting, the USS Alabama Battleship Memorial Park provides an unforgettable experience for visitors of all ages.

Activities and attractions for different age groups:

1. Young children (2-8):
    - Exploring the park's playground and picnic areas for outdoor play and family time
    - Participating in the "Junior Crew" program, which offers age-appropriate activities and a special tour of the battleship
    - Enjoying the park's green spaces and watching the aircraft and other military vehicles on display
2. Older children and teenagers (9-18):
    - Touring the USS Alabama battleship and learning about life aboard a WWII-era naval vessel
    - Exploring the USS Drum submarine and

discovering the unique challenges of underwater warfare
- Visiting the Aircraft Pavilion to see a variety of vintage military aircraft up close
- Participating in educational scavenger hunts or guided tours tailored to their interests and age group

3. Adults:
- Gaining a deeper understanding of WWII history and the role of the USS Alabama through exhibits and guided tours
- Appreciating the engineering and technological innovations that made the battleship a formidable warship
- Attending special events, such as the annual "Living History Crew Drill" or the "Battleship 12K and 5K Run"
- Enjoying the park's scenic location on Mobile Bay and taking advantage of photo opportunities

Amenities and accessibility:

- The park offers ample parking, including designated spots for visitors with disabilities
- Restrooms, water fountains, and a gift shop are located on-site for visitor convenience
- The park has picnic areas with tables and benches for visitors to enjoy meals or snacks
- While most of the battleship is not wheelchair accessible due to its historic nature, the park offers an ADA-compliant tour that covers the main deck and other accessible areas
- The park's grounds, including the memorials and exhibits,

are generally accessible, with paved paths and ramps

Educational programs and tours: The USS Alabama Battleship Memorial Park offers a variety of educational programs and tours, including:

- Self-guided tours of the USS Alabama battleship and USS Drum submarine using provided maps and information
- Guided tours led by knowledgeable docents who share stories and insights about the ships and their crews
- Educational programs for school groups that align with state curriculum standards
- Overnight camping programs that allow scouts and youth groups to sleep aboard the battleship and experience life as a sailor
- Special events and presentations that focus on specific aspects of WWII history or naval technology

Nearby attractions and accommodations:

- The park is located just minutes from downtown Mobile, which offers a variety of dining, shopping, and lodging options
- Other nearby attractions include Bellingrath Gardens and Home, the Mobile Carnival Museum, and the GulfQuest National Maritime Museum
- The park is also conveniently located near popular Gulf Coast beaches and vacation destinations, such as Gulf Shores and Orange Beach

Tips for visiting:

- Allow at least 2-3 hours to fully explore the park and its attractions

- Wear comfortable walking shoes and be prepared for stairs and narrow passageways when touring the battleship
- Bring sunscreen, hats, and water, especially during the summer months, as much of the park is outdoors
- Check the park's website or social media pages for information on special events, programs, and promotions
- Consider purchasing a souvenir or making a donation to support the park's preservation and educational efforts

The USS Alabama Battleship Memorial Park is a must-visit destination for families seeking an immersive and educational experience that brings history to life. By providing a fascinating glimpse into the world of WWII-era naval warfare, as well as opportunities for outdoor recreation and family bonding, the park offers a well-rounded and engaging experience that appeals to visitors of all ages and interests. Whether you're a history buff, a military enthusiast, or simply looking for a unique and meaningful family outing, the USS Alabama Battleship Memorial Park is sure to leave a lasting impression and provide valuable insights into our nation's past.

Barber Vintage Motorsports Museum

(Birmingham)

Address: 6030 Barber Motorsports Pkwy, Birmingham, AL 35094

Phone: (205) 699-7275

Hours: Monday-Saturday 10 AM - 5 PM, Sunday 12 PM - 5 PM

Admission: Adults $16, Children (4-16) $6, Children under 4 free

The Barber Vintage Motorsports Museum is a fantastic destination for families who appreciate the artistry, history, and excitement of motorcycles and motorsports. With its extensive collection, engaging exhibits, and on-site racetrack, the museum offers a unique and thrilling experience that appeals to visitors of all ages.

Activities and attractions for different age groups:

1. Young children (2-8):
    - Exploring the museum's "Scavenger Hunt" activity, which encourages children to find specific motorcycles and learn fun facts about them
    - Participating in hands-on activities, such as the "Build-a-Bike" station, where children can create their own motorcycle using magnetic parts
    - Enjoying the museum's play area, which features ride-on toys and other interactive elements
2. Older children and teenagers (9-18):
    - Discovering the science and technology behind motorcycles through interactive exhibits and demonstrations

- ○ Participating in the museum's "Pit Crew Challenge," which tests teamwork and problem-solving skills in a race-themed setting
- ○ Attending youth-focused workshops and classes that teach basic motorcycle maintenance and safety skills
- ○ Watching live motorsports events at the museum's on-site racetrack

3. Adults:
   - ○ Admiring the museum's extensive collection of vintage motorcycles and race cars, representing over 100 years of automotive history
   - ○ Learning about the cultural impact and evolution of motorcycles through guided tours and exhibits
   - ○ Attending special events, such as vintage motorcycle shows, book signings, and meet-and-greets with industry experts
   - ○ Participating in adult-oriented workshops and classes, such as motorcycle restoration or photography

Amenities and accessibility:

- The museum offers ample parking, including designated spots for visitors with disabilities
- Restrooms and a cafe are located on-site for visitor convenience
- The museum's main exhibit areas are wheelchair accessible, with elevators and ramps providing access to all levels
- Guided tours and audio guides are available for visitors who prefer a more structured experience
- The museum has a gift shop featuring motorcycle-related items, books, and souvenirs

Educational programs and events: The Barber Vintage Motorsports Museum offers a variety of educational programs and events, including:

- Guided tours led by knowledgeable docents who share stories and insights about the museum's collection
- Workshops and classes that focus on motorcycle history, technology, and maintenance
- Youth programs that introduce children to the world of motorcycles and motorsports in a safe and engaging way
- Special exhibits and events that showcase specific aspects of motorcycle culture or racing history
- Collaborative programs with local schools and community organizations to promote STEM education and career opportunities

Nearby attractions and accommodations:

- The museum is located near the heart of Birmingham, which offers a wide range of dining, shopping, and lodging options
- Other nearby attractions include the Birmingham Zoo, the McWane Science Center, and the Birmingham Civil Rights Institute
- The museum is also conveniently located near popular outdoor recreation areas, such as Oak Mountain State Park and Red Mountain Park

Tips for visiting:

- Allow at least 2-3 hours to fully explore the museum's exhibits and attractions
- Check the museum's website or social media pages for

information on special events, programs, and promotions

- Consider purchasing a souvenir or making a donation to support the museum's preservation and educational efforts
- If you're interested in watching a live motorsports event, be sure to check the museum's event calendar and plan your visit accordingly
- For a more immersive experience, consider taking a guided tour or participating in one of the museum's workshops or classes

The Barber Vintage Motorsports Museum is a must-visit destination for families who appreciate the artistry, innovation, and excitement of motorcycles and motorsports. By providing a unique blend of history, technology, and hands-on experiences, the museum offers a captivating and educational experience that sparks curiosity and imagination in visitors of all ages. Whether you're a lifelong motorcycle enthusiast or simply looking for a fun and engaging family outing, the Barber Vintage Motorsports Museum promises an unforgettable adventure that celebrates the spirit of the open road.

LAKEPOINT RESORT
STATE PARK

Lakepoint State Park

(Eufaula)

Address: 104 Lakepoint Resort Rd, Eufaula, AL 36027

Phone: (334) 687-8011

Hours: Park grounds open daily from 7 AM to Sunset

Admission: $5 per vehicle

Lakepoint State Park is a wonderful destination for families looking to unwind, enjoy outdoor activities, and create lasting memories amidst the beautiful natural surroundings of Lake Eufaula. With its diverse recreational opportunities, scenic beauty, and well-maintained facilities, the park offers a perfect getaway for nature lovers and outdoor enthusiasts of all ages.

Activities and attractions for different age groups:

1. Young children (2-8):
    - Playing on the park's sandy beach and splashing in the shallow waters of Lake Eufaula
    - Exploring the park's playground and picnic areas for outdoor fun and family time
    - Participating in nature-themed scavenger hunts or guided walks led by park rangers
2. Older children and teenagers (9-18):
    - Fishing in Lake Eufaula for bass, crappie, catfish, and other species (fishing license required for ages 12 and up)
    - Swimming, kayaking, or paddleboarding in the designated areas of the lake

- Hiking the park's trails to discover local flora, fauna, and scenic views
- Biking on the park's paved roads or exploring the surrounding area on two wheels

3. Adults:
   - Boating, water-skiing, or jet-skiing on Lake Eufaula (boat rentals available at the park's marina)
   - Golfing at the park's scenic 18-hole championship golf course
   - Relaxing on the beach, fishing pier, or in the park's picturesque picnic areas
   - Birdwatching and wildlife viewing along the park's trails and natural areas

Amenities and facilities:

- The park offers a variety of lodging options, including lakeside cabins, cottages, and a modern campground with RV sites and tent sites
- The park's marina provides boat rentals, fishing supplies, and a launch ramp for private boats
- A beach area, fishing pier, and picnic pavilions are available for visitor use
- The park has a camp store that sells snacks, drinks, ice, and basic camping supplies
- An 18-hole championship golf course and pro shop are located within the park

Accessibility:

- The park's main facilities, including the lodge, restaurant, and some cabins, are wheelchair accessible

- Some of the park's trails and picnic areas are accessible, with paved or graded surfaces
- The park offers accessible parking spaces and restrooms in key areas
- Visitors with specific accessibility needs should contact the park office for more information and assistance

Nearby attractions and points of interest:

- The city of Eufaula, known for its historic homes, charming downtown, and annual pilgrimage event
- The Eufaula National Wildlife Refuge, which offers additional opportunities for wildlife viewing, hiking, and fishing
- The Creek Indian Casino, located just a short drive from the park, for those interested in gaming and entertainment
- Other nearby state parks, such as Florence Marina State Park and George T. Bagby State Park, for additional outdoor recreation and sightseeing opportunities

Tips for visiting:

- Make reservations for lodging or campsites well in advance, especially during peak seasons like summer and holidays
- Check the park's website or social media pages for information on special events, programs, and promotions
- Bring sunscreen, insect repellent, and appropriate clothing for outdoor activities and changing weather conditions
- Be mindful of park rules and regulations, including speed limits, quiet hours, and pet policies
- Take advantage of the park's educational programs, guided tours, and wildlife exhibits to learn more about the area's natural and cultural heritage

Lakepoint State Park is a must-visit destination for families seeking a fun, relaxing, and nature-filled getaway in the heart of Alabama's lake country. With its stunning location on Lake Eufaula, diverse recreational opportunities, and well-maintained facilities, the park offers a perfect backdrop for creating unforgettable family memories and fostering a deep appreciation for the great outdoors. Whether you're interested in fishing, boating, hiking, or simply enjoying the peaceful surroundings, Lakepoint State Park promises a truly rejuvenating and enjoyable experience for visitors of all ages.

Ripley's Aquarium

(Birmingham)

Address: 1608 EastChase Pkwy, Huntsville, AL 35806

Phone: (866) 241-3700

Hours: Daily from 10 AM to 8 PM

Admission: Adults $27.99, Children (6-11) $16.99, Children under 6 free

Ripley's Aquarium in Birmingham is an incredible destination that immerses families in the wonders of the aquatic world. With its stunning exhibits, interactive experiences, and commitment to education and conservation, the aquarium offers a fun-filled and informative day out for visitors of all ages.

Activities and attractions for different age groups:

1. Young children (2-6):
    - Exploring the "Ray Bay" touch tank, where children can gently touch and learn about friendly stingrays and small sharks
    - Enjoying the colorful and vibrant "Tropical Rainforest" exhibit, featuring poison dart frogs, piranhas, and other fascinating creatures
    - Participating in the "Mermaid & Pirate Dive Show," an entertaining and interactive performance that combines storytelling, music, and underwater acrobatics
2. Older children and teenagers (7-18):
    - Discovering the "Shark Lagoon," a mesmerizing

exhibit featuring several species of sharks and a thrilling underwater shark tunnel

- Exploring the "Ocean Realm" gallery, which showcases the incredible diversity of marine life, from giant octopuses to delicate seahorses
- Attending educational presentations and animal encounters, such as the "Penguin Encounter" or the "Stingray Experience," to learn more about these fascinating creatures and their habitats

3. Adults:

- Marveling at the aquarium's extensive collection of marine life and learning about the importance of ocean conservation
- Participating in behind-the-scenes tours to gain insight into the aquarium's operations, animal care, and research efforts
- Enjoying the aquarium's special events, such as "Date Night" or "Paint Nite," which offer unique experiences and a chance to unwind in a stunning setting
- Shopping for unique gifts and souvenirs at the aquarium's gift shop, which offers a wide selection of marine-themed items

Amenities and accessibility:

- The aquarium is fully wheelchair accessible, with elevators, ramps, and wide pathways throughout the facility
- Restrooms, including family restrooms and changing tables, are located conveniently throughout the aquarium
- The aquarium offers a cafe and gift shop for snacks, meals, and souvenirs
- Strollers are permitted inside the aquarium, and stroller

parking is available near the entrance

- Complimentary Wi-Fi is available throughout the aquarium

Educational programs and experiences: Ripley's Aquarium offers a variety of educational programs and experiences for families and students, including:

- School field trips and homeschool programs that align with state and national curriculum standards
- Summer camps and workshops that provide hands-on learning experiences and behind-the-scenes access
- Animal encounters and interactive presentations led by knowledgeable aquarium staff
- Dive shows and feedings that showcase the aquarium's animals and their natural behaviors
- Outreach programs and virtual learning opportunities for schools and community groups

Conservation and research efforts: Ripley's Aquarium is committed to ocean conservation and actively participates in research and conservation efforts, such as:

- Partnering with organizations like the Association of Zoos and Aquariums (AZA) to support marine conservation projects and initiatives
- Participating in breeding programs for endangered species and contributing to species survival plans
- Conducting research on animal behavior, husbandry, and conservation to improve the well-being of aquatic life both in the aquarium and in the wild
- Educating visitors about the importance of ocean conservation and inspiring them to take action in their

daily lives

Tips for visiting:

- Purchase tickets online in advance to save time and ensure availability, especially during peak seasons and holidays
- Plan to spend at least 2-3 hours exploring the aquarium's exhibits and attending shows and presentations
- Check the daily schedule for animal feedings, dive shows, and educational presentations to make the most of your visit
- Bring a camera to capture your favorite moments and memories, but be mindful of flash photography and respect the animals' well-being
- Consider purchasing a souvenir or making a donation to support the aquarium's conservation and education efforts

Ripley's Aquarium in Birmingham is a must-visit destination for families looking to explore the incredible world beneath the waves. With its stunning exhibits, interactive experiences, and commitment to education and conservation, the aquarium provides a fun and informative day out that sparks curiosity, inspires learning, and fosters a deep appreciation for the beauty and diversity of aquatic life. Whether you're a marine enthusiast or simply looking for a unique and engaging family activity, Ripley's Aquarium promises an unforgettable adventure that will leave you in awe of the wonders of the ocean.

Tuscaloosa Children's Hands-On Museum

(Tuscaloosa)

Address: 1211 Denny Way, Tuscaloosa, AL 35401

Phone: (205) 349-4235

Hours: Tuesday-Saturday 10 AM - 4 PM, Sunday 1 PM - 4 PM (Closed Mondays)

Admission: Adults $8, Children (2-12) $8, Children under 2 free

The Tuscaloosa Children's Hands-On Museum is a fantastic destination for families with young children, offering a wide range of interactive exhibits and engaging activities that promote learning through play. With its focus on creativity, exploration, and discovery, the museum provides a stimulating environment that encourages children to learn and grow while having fun.

Activities and attractions for different age groups:

1. Toddlers and preschoolers (2-5):
    - Exploring the "Itty Bitty City" exhibit, which features a miniature town designed for imaginative play and role-playing
    - Engaging in sensory play at the "Water Works" and "Sand Play" stations, which promote fine motor skills and tactile exploration
    - Enjoying story time and age-appropriate crafts in the "Art Studio"
2. Elementary school-aged children (6-12):
    - Discovering the principles of science, technology,

engineering, and math (STEM) through hands-on exhibits in the "Science Lab"
- Creating and building in the "Construction Zone," which offers a variety of materials and tools for open-ended play
- Participating in the museum's "Challenge of the Week," which presents a new problem-solving activity each week to encourage critical thinking and collaboration

3. Adults and caregivers:
   - Engaging in play-based learning alongside their children, fostering bonding and shared experiences
   - Attending parent workshops and special events that provide insights into child development and strategies for supporting learning at home
   - Relaxing in the museum's "Grown-Up Getaway" area, which offers comfortable seating and resources for parents and caregivers

Amenities and accessibility:

- The museum offers a small gift shop with educational toys, books, and souvenirs
- Restrooms and changing tables are available for family convenience
- The museum is wheelchair accessible, with ramps and wide pathways for easy navigation
- Sensory backpacks containing noise-reducing headphones, fidget toys, and other resources are available for children with sensory sensitivities
- The museum provides lockers for storing personal belongings during your visit

Educational programs and events: The Tuscaloosa Children's Hands-On Museum offers a variety of educational programs and events throughout the year, including:

- Field trip programs for school and homeschool groups, tailored to different age groups and learning objectives
- Summer camps and workshops that provide in-depth exploration of specific themes or subjects
- "Museum After Dark" events, which offer special evening hours and activities for families
- Seasonal events and celebrations, such as "Noon Year's Eve" and "Halloween Spooktacular"

Membership and support: The museum offers membership options for families and individuals, which provide benefits such as:

- Unlimited admission to the museum for a year
- Discounts on birthday parties, camps, and special events
- Reciprocal admission to other participating children's museums across the country
- Invitations to member-only events and previews
- Supporting the museum's mission and educational initiatives through financial contributions

Tips for visiting:

- Plan to spend at least 2-3 hours exploring the museum's exhibits and activities
- Encourage your children to take their time, ask questions, and engage with the exhibits in their own way
- Bring a lunch or snack to enjoy in the museum's designated eating areas, as outside food is not permitted in the exhibit spaces

- Consider visiting during off-peak hours (weekday afternoons or Sunday) for a more relaxed experience
- Check the museum's website or social media pages for information on current exhibits, programs, and special events

The Tuscaloosa Children's Hands-On Museum is a must-visit destination for families seeking a fun, educational, and engaging experience that nurtures a love for learning and discovery. By providing a diverse array of interactive exhibits, programs, and amenities designed specifically for young learners, the museum creates a welcoming and inclusive environment that encourages children to explore, create, and grow. Whether you're a local family or visiting from out of town, the Tuscaloosa Children's Hands-On Museum promises a memorable and enriching experience that will spark your child's imagination and curiosity.

Priceville Pumpkin Patch

(Priceville)

Address: 3000 Brock Rd, Priceville, AL 35603

Phone: (256) 355-7034

Hours: Seasonal, typically open from late September to late October

Admission: Prices vary based on activities

The Priceville Pumpkin Patch is a wonderful destination for families looking to embrace the spirit of autumn and create lasting memories together. With its wide array of activities and attractions, the pumpkin patch offers a fun and festive experience for visitors of all ages.

Activities and attractions for different age groups:

1. Toddlers and preschoolers (2-5):
    - Exploring the pumpkin patch and selecting their very own pumpkin to take home
    - Enjoying a gentle hayride around the farm, taking in the sights and sounds of autumn
    - Petting and feeding friendly animals at the petting zoo, such as goats, sheep, and rabbits
    - Playing in the "Corn Box," a large sandbox filled with kernels of corn for sensory play
2. Elementary school-aged children (6-12):
    - Navigating the twists and turns of the corn maze, solving clues and puzzles along the way
    - Taking part in the "Pumpkin Launch," using a giant slingshot to launch pumpkins at targets

- Jumping and playing on the "Hay Mountain," a large stack of hay bales for climbing and exploring
- Participating in fall-themed games and activities, such as pumpkin painting and scarecrow building

3. Teenagers and adults:
    - Challenging each other to complete the corn maze in record time
    - Enjoying a leisurely hayride and taking in the beautiful autumn scenery
    - Exploring the haunted trail (if available) for a thrilling and spooky experience
    - Capturing family photos among the picturesque pumpkin patch and fall decorations

Amenities and accessibility:

- The pumpkin patch offers restroom facilities and handwashing stations for visitor convenience
- Food and beverage options, such as concessions or food trucks, may be available during peak hours
- Some areas of the pumpkin patch may have uneven or muddy terrain, so visitors should wear appropriate footwear and be prepared for walking on unpaved surfaces
- Visitors with mobility concerns should contact the pumpkin patch directly to inquire about accessibility accommodations

Special events and offerings: The Priceville Pumpkin Patch may offer special events and offerings throughout the season, such as:

- "Flashlight Nights" or "Moonlight Madness," where visitors can explore the corn maze and other attractions after dark
- Live entertainment, such as music performances or

storytelling sessions

- Food and craft vendors showcasing local products and autumn-themed items
- Educational demonstrations or workshops related to farming, agriculture, or fall crafts

Tips for visiting:

- Check the pumpkin patch's website or social media pages for the most up-to-date information on hours, admission prices, and available activities
- Wear comfortable, weather-appropriate clothing and sturdy shoes for walking on uneven surfaces
- Bring sunscreen, hats, and water, especially during warm autumn days
- Consider visiting on weekdays or during off-peak hours to avoid crowds and ensure a more relaxed experience
- Be respectful of the pumpkin patch's rules and guidelines, such as not littering and being gentle with animals in the petting zoo

Nearby attractions and accommodations:

- The town of Priceville and the surrounding area offer various dining options, from local cafes to chain restaurants
- Visitors can explore nearby attractions, such as the Wheeler National Wildlife Refuge or the historic downtown district of Decatur
- Accommodations, such as hotels and bed & breakfasts, can be found in the nearby cities of Decatur and Huntsville for those looking to extend their stay in the area

The Priceville Pumpkin Patch is a must-visit destination for families seeking a quintessential autumn experience filled with fun, laughter, and cherished memories. By offering a diverse array of activities and attractions that cater to various ages and interests, the pumpkin patch ensures that every visitor can find something to enjoy and celebrate the magic of the fall season. Whether you're looking to pick the perfect pumpkin, navigate a challenging corn maze, or simply soak in the beauty of the changing leaves, the Priceville Pumpkin Patch promises a delightful and memorable day out for the whole family.

HANK WILLIAMS
MUSEUM

Hank Williams Museum

(Montgomery)

Address: 850 Avalon St, Montgomery, AL 36107

Phone: (334) 262-8165

Hours: Monday-Saturday 9 AM - 4 PM, Sunday 1 PM - 4 PM

Admission: Adults $6, Children (6-17) $4, Children under 6 free

The Hank Williams Museum is a fascinating destination that offers families a unique opportunity to explore the life and legacy of one of America's most beloved and influential country music stars. With its comprehensive exhibits, interactive experiences, and dedication to preserving Williams' memory, the museum provides an engaging and educational experience for visitors of all ages.

Activities and attractions for different age groups:

1. Elementary school-aged children (6-12):
    - Discovering the story of Hank Williams' life through interactive exhibits and displays designed to engage young learners
    - Exploring the museum's collection of memorabilia, including Williams' guitars, stage costumes, and personal belongings
    - Participating in the museum's scavenger hunt, which encourages children to search for specific items and learn fun facts about Williams' life and career
2. Teenagers (13-17):
    - Gaining a deeper understanding of Hank

Williams' impact on country music and American popular culture through the museum's informative exhibits and audio-visual presentations
- Exploring the social and historical context of Williams' life and times, including the challenges and triumphs he faced as a musician and public figure
- Engaging with the museum's interactive elements, such as the recording studio, where visitors can experience the thrill of performing one of Williams' classic songs

3. Adults:
- Immersing themselves in the rich history and cultural significance of Hank Williams' music and legacy
- Appreciating the museum's extensive collection of rare artifacts, photographs, and memorabilia that provide a intimate glimpse into Williams' personal and professional life
- Attending special events, such as live music performances, lectures, or book signings, that celebrate Williams' enduring impact on country music and American culture

Accessibility and amenities:

- The museum is wheelchair accessible, with ramps and wide doorways to accommodate visitors with mobility needs
- Restrooms are available for visitor convenience
- The museum's gift shop offers a wide selection of Hank Williams-related merchandise, including books, CDs, and souvenirs

Guided tours and educational programs: The Hank Williams Museum offers guided tours and educational programs that provide a more in-depth and personalized experience for visitors, including:

- Guided tours led by knowledgeable docents who share stories, insights, and anecdotes about Williams' life and career
- Educational programs for school groups that align with state curriculum standards and provide hands-on learning experiences
- Special tours and programs for music enthusiasts, historians, and researchers interested in exploring specific aspects of Williams' legacy

Nearby attractions and accommodations:

- The museum is located in downtown Montgomery, within walking distance of other notable attractions, such as the Alabama State Capitol and the Montgomery Riverfront Park
- Visitors can explore the Hank Williams Memorial, a life-sized statue of the singer located just a short drive from the museum
- A variety of dining and lodging options are available in the surrounding area, catering to various budgets and preferences

Tips for visiting:

- Allow at least 1-2 hours to fully explore the museum's exhibits and attractions
- Check the museum's website or social media pages for information on special events, programs, and promotions

- Consider purchasing a souvenir or making a donation to support the museum's ongoing efforts to preserve and promote Hank Williams' legacy
- For a more immersive experience, consider planning your visit to coincide with one of the museum's live music events or special programs

The Hank Williams Museum is a must-visit destination for families who want to explore the rich history and cultural significance of one of America's most iconic and influential musicians. By providing a comprehensive and engaging look at Williams' life, music, and legacy, the museum offers a unique and memorable experience that appeals to visitors of all ages and backgrounds. Whether you're a die-hard country music fan or simply curious about this legendary figure, the Hank Williams Museum promises a fascinating journey through the world of a true American original.

AMERICAN
VILLAGE
WELCOME
OPEN TO THE PUBLIC

American Village

(Montevallo)

Address: 3727 Highway 119, Montevallo, AL 35115

Phone: (205) 665-3535

Hours: Monday-Saturday 10 AM - 4 PM, Sunday 12 PM - 4 PM

Admission: Adults $9, Children (4-18) $6, Children under 4 free

The American Village is a fantastic destination for families looking to immerse themselves in the history and founding principles of the United States. With its engaging living history demonstrations, interactive exhibits, and educational programs, the village offers a unique and memorable experience that brings the past to life and encourages visitors to reflect on the values that have shaped the nation.

Activities and attractions for different age groups:

1. Elementary school-aged children (6-12):
   - Participating in hands-on activities and games that teach about colonial life, such as candle-making, quill pen writing, and hoop rolling
   - Attending a Revolutionary-era school session to experience education in the 18th century
   - Engaging with costumed interpreters portraying historical figures, such as George Washington or Betsy Ross, and asking questions about their lives and times
2. Teenagers (13-18):
   - Exploring the village's replica buildings and

exhibits to gain a deeper understanding of the political, social, and economic factors that influenced the founding of the United States
- Participating in interactive debates and discussions that encourage critical thinking about the nation's founding principles and their relevance today
- Attending special events and programs that focus on specific aspects of American history, such as the Revolutionary War or the drafting of the Constitution

3. Adults:
- Gaining new insights into the historical context and significance of the events and ideas that shaped the nation's founding
- Appreciating the attention to detail and historical accuracy in the village's replica buildings, costumes, and exhibits
- Engaging in thought-provoking discussions and debates with costumed interpreters and other visitors about the enduring legacy of the American Revolution and its impact on contemporary society

Accessibility and amenities:

- The American Village is wheelchair accessible, with paved paths and ramps throughout the grounds
- Restrooms and water fountains are located throughout the village for visitor convenience
- The village's gift shop offers a selection of books, souvenirs, and educational materials related to American history and the founding era

Educational programs and special events: The American Village offers a variety of educational programs and special events throughout the year, including:

- Field trip programs for school groups that align with state curriculum standards and provide hands-on learning experiences
- Homeschool days that offer special activities and programs tailored to the needs and interests of homeschooling families
- Summer camps and workshops that provide in-depth exploration of specific historical topics or skills, such as archaeology or 18th-century music
- Special events and celebrations, such as the annual Independence Day festival or the Veterans Day commemoration, that honor the nation's history and heritage

Nearby attractions and accommodations:

- The American Village is located near the historic town of Montevallo, which offers a variety of dining options and small shops to explore
- Visitors can take a short drive to the town of Calera to visit the Heart of Dixie Railroad Museum, which offers train rides and exhibits on Alabama's railroad history
- The Birmingham area, located just 45 minutes away, offers a wide range of accommodations, from budget-friendly hotels to upscale resorts, as well as additional cultural and recreational attractions

Tips for visiting:

- Plan to spend at least 2-3 hours at the village to fully experience the exhibits, demonstrations, and activities
- Check the village's website or social media pages for information on special events, programs, and promotions
- Wear comfortable walking shoes and weather-appropriate clothing, as much of the village is outdoors and involves walking on unpaved surfaces
- Consider bringing a picnic lunch to enjoy on the village green or at one of the nearby picnic areas
- Encourage children to ask questions and engage with the costumed interpreters to maximize their learning experience

The American Village is a must-visit destination for families who want to explore the rich history and founding principles of the United States in an engaging, interactive, and thought-provoking way. By providing a unique blend of living history demonstrations, educational programs, and immersive experiences, the village offers a transformative journey that brings the past to life and encourages visitors of all ages to reflect on the values and ideals that have shaped the nation. Whether you're a history buff, an educator, or simply a curious learner, the American Village promises an unforgettable adventure that will inspire a deeper appreciation for America's heritage and the ongoing struggle to "form a more perfect Union."

Bryant-Denny Stadium

(Tuscaloosa)

Address: 292 Evergreen Ln, Tuscaloosa, AL 35401

Phone: (205) 348-3600

Hours: Open on game days and for tours

Admission: Ticket prices vary for games, tours are $10 for adults, $8 for children

Bryant-Denny Stadium is a must-visit destination for families who love sports, history, and the excitement of a big college football game. With its impressive size, storied history, and electrifying atmosphere, the stadium offers a unique and unforgettable experience that appeals to visitors of all ages.

Activities and attractions for different age groups:

1. Elementary school-aged children (6-12):
    - Experiencing the thrill and excitement of a live college football game, complete with cheering crowds, marching bands, and mascots
    - Participating in pre-game activities, such as face painting, cheerleader meet-and-greets, or interactive fan zones
    - Exploring the stadium during guided tours, learning about its history and imagining what it's like to be a player or coach on game day
2. Teenagers (13-18):
    - Appreciating the skill, athleticism, and dedication of the college football players and coaches

- Learning about the rich history and traditions of the Alabama Crimson Tide football program, including its many championship seasons and legendary players
- Experiencing the camaraderie and school spirit of a major college football event, which can inspire a sense of pride and connection to the university and its community

3. Adults:
- Enjoying the excitement and nostalgia of a college football game, whether as a long-time fan or a newcomer to the sport
- Tailgating with friends and family before the game, savoring delicious food, beverages, and the festive atmosphere
- Taking a guided tour of the stadium to gain a behind-the-scenes look at the facilities, press box, and locker rooms, and learning about the stadium's architecture and technological features

Accessibility and amenities:

- Bryant-Denny Stadium offers accessible seating, restrooms, and parking for visitors with disabilities
- Concessions stands and restrooms are located throughout the stadium for visitor convenience
- The stadium has a clear bag policy and security measures in place to ensure the safety and security of all visitors
- Strollers and large bags are not permitted inside the stadium, but a limited number of stroller check-in areas may be available

Guided tours and special events: Bryant-Denny Stadium offers guided tours and special events throughout the year, including:

- Guided tours that provide a behind-the-scenes look at the stadium's facilities, history, and operations
- Special events, such as fan day or autograph sessions, where visitors can meet players and coaches
- Youth football clinics and camps that offer aspiring players the chance to learn from college coaches and athletes
- Private events and rentals, such as weddings, corporate meetings, or banquets, that utilize the stadium's unique setting and amenities

Nearby attractions and accommodations:

- The University of Alabama campus offers a variety of attractions, such as the Paul W. Bryant Museum, which showcases the history of Crimson Tide athletics
- The Tuscaloosa area offers a range of dining, shopping, and entertainment options, from local restaurants and boutiques to movie theaters and parks
- Accommodations near the stadium include hotels, motels, and bed & breakfasts, catering to various budgets and preferences

Tips for visiting:

- Check the stadium's website or social media pages for information on game schedules, ticket sales, and special events
- Plan to arrive early on game days to allow time for parking, tailgating, and navigating the crowds
- Wear comfortable, weather-appropriate clothing and

shoes, as the stadium is open-air and involves walking and climbing stairs
- Be respectful of the stadium's rules and regulations, including the clear bag policy and prohibited items list
- Have fun, show good sportsmanship, and enjoy the unique experience of a college football game at one of the nation's most iconic stadiums

Bryant-Denny Stadium is a landmark destination that offers families a thrilling and memorable experience, whether they are die-hard college football fans or simply curious visitors. By combining the excitement of a live sporting event with the rich history and traditions of the Alabama Crimson Tide, the stadium provides an engaging and inspiring glimpse into the world of college athletics and the enduring spirit of competition and camaraderie. Whether you're cheering on the home team, exploring the stadium's fascinating features, or simply soaking in the electric atmosphere, a visit to Bryant-Denny Stadium promises an unforgettable adventure that will leave you with a deeper appreciation for the power and passion of sports.

CHATTAHOOCHEE
NATURE CENTER
ENTRANCE

Chattahoochee Nature Center

(Phenix City)

Address: 489 Woodruff Farm Rd, Phenix City, AL 36867

Phone: (334) 705-6140

Hours: Tuesday-Sunday 10 AM - 5 PM (Closed Mondays)

Admission: Adults $8, Children (3-12) $5, Children under 3 free

The Chattahoochee Nature Center is a wonderful destination for families looking to connect with nature, learn about the environment, and enjoy outdoor recreational activities together. With its diverse habitats, educational programs, and scenic beauty, the center offers a unique and enriching experience for visitors of all ages.

Activities and attractions for different age groups:

1. Toddlers and preschoolers (2-5):
    - Exploring the center's "Discovery Room," which features hands-on nature exhibits, live animal displays, and interactive play areas
    - Participating in the "Nature Nuggets" program, which offers age-appropriate nature walks, stories, and crafts led by experienced naturalists
    - Enjoying the center's outdoor play areas, which include a nature-themed playground and picnic tables
2. Elementary school-aged children (6-12):
    - Hiking the center's trails, such as the Woodruff Farm Trail or the Wetland Walkway, to observe

plants, animals, and natural habitats up close
- Attending the center's "Junior Naturalist" program, which teaches outdoor skills, environmental science, and nature appreciation through hands-on activities and field trips
- Participating in guided bird walks, pond studies, or other themed nature programs designed for curious young minds

3. Teenagers and adults:
- Exploring the center's longer hiking trails, such as the 3-mile Chattahoochee River Trail, which offers scenic views and opportunities for wildlife spotting
- Attending workshops and lectures on topics such as nature photography, organic gardening, or local history and culture
- Volunteering with the center's habitat restoration projects, trail maintenance, or educational programs to support conservation efforts and gain valuable experience

Amenities and accessibility:

- The center has a visitor center with restrooms, a gift shop, and a small exhibit area
- Picnic tables and benches are located throughout the grounds for visitors to enjoy meals or rest
- Some trails are wheelchair and stroller accessible, with boardwalks and crushed gravel surfaces, while others are more rugged and may require sturdy footwear
- The center offers ample parking and is conveniently located near major highways and the cities of Phenix City and Columbus, GA

Educational programs and events: The Chattahoochee Nature Center offers a wide range of educational programs and events throughout the year, including:

- School field trips and homeschool programs aligned with state curriculum standards
- Summer camps and school break camps that provide immersive nature experiences and outdoor skill-building
- Family programs, such as night hikes, campfire stories, or live animal presentations
- Community events, such as the annual "Butterfly Festival" or "Owl-O-Ween" celebration
- Workshops and classes for adults on topics like birdwatching, nature journaling, or sustainable living practices

Nearby attractions and accommodations:

- The Phenix City Riverwalk, located just minutes from the nature center, offers scenic views of the Chattahoochee River and additional recreational opportunities
- The National Infantry Museum and Soldier Center, located across the river in Columbus, GA, provides a fascinating look at U.S. military history
- Accommodations in Phenix City and Columbus include a variety of hotels, motels, and bed & breakfasts to suit different budgets and preferences

Tips for visiting:

- Check the center's website or social media pages for up-to-date information on hours, programs, and events
- Wear comfortable, weather-appropriate clothing and

sturdy shoes for hiking and outdoor activities
- Bring insect repellent, sunscreen, water, and snacks, especially during warm months
- Consider bringing binoculars, a camera, or a nature journal to enhance your experience and record your observations
- Be respectful of wildlife and natural habitats by following "Leave No Trace" principles and staying on designated trails

The Chattahoochee Nature Center is a must-visit destination for families seeking to foster a love of nature, outdoor recreation, and environmental stewardship. By providing a diverse array of habitats, trails, and educational opportunities, the center offers a unique and immersive experience that encourages visitors to explore, learn, and appreciate the natural world. Whether you're a local resident or a visitor to the Phenix City area, the Chattahoochee Nature Center promises an unforgettable adventure that will inspire a deeper connection to the beauty and wonder of the great outdoors.

Bogue's Buddy Art Park

(Montgomery)

Address: 2220 Highland Ave, Montgomery, AL 36107

Phone: (334) 625-4491

Hours: Park grounds open daily from dawn to dusk

Admission: Free

Bogue's Buddy Art Park is a fantastic destination for families looking to explore the intersection of art, nature, and imaginative play. With its interactive sculptures, educational elements, and inviting green spaces, the park offers a unique and engaging experience that encourages creativity, curiosity, and appreciation for the arts.

Activities and attractions for different age groups:

1. Toddlers and preschoolers (2-5):
    - Exploring the park's colorful and tactile sculptures, which encourage sensory exploration and imaginative play
    - Enjoying the park's playground equipment, such as swings, slides, and climbing structures
    - Participating in age-appropriate art activities or scavenger hunts designed to engage young minds
2. Elementary school-aged children (6-12):
    - Interacting with the park's diverse array of sculptures, learning about the artists' inspirations and techniques
    - Discovering the educational messages and themes embedded in the artwork, such as environmental

conservation or community pride

○ Creating their own art inspired by the park's installations, using materials provided by the park or brought from home

3. Teenagers and adults:

○ Appreciating the creativity, skill, and vision of the local artists who contributed to the park's diverse collection of sculptures

○ Engaging in discussions about the role of public art in enhancing community spaces and sparking dialogue

○ Relaxing in the park's peaceful green spaces, enjoying a picnic or a quiet moment surrounded by art and nature

Amenities and accessibility:

- The park offers benches, picnic tables, and shade structures for visitor comfort and convenience
- Restrooms and drinking fountains are available on-site
- The park's paths and playground areas are wheelchair and stroller accessible, with smooth surfaces and gentle inclines
- Ample parking is available nearby, with designated spaces for visitors with disabilities

Educational programs and events: Bogue's Buddy Art Park hosts a variety of educational programs and events throughout the year, including:

- Artist-led workshops and demonstrations that teach art techniques and concepts to children and families
- Guided tours and scavenger hunts that highlight the park's sculptures and their educational themes

- Community art projects that encourage visitors to contribute to collaborative installations or murals
- Seasonal events and celebrations that showcase local talent and bring the community together around art and creativity

Nearby attractions and amenities:

- The park is located in the charming Old Cloverdale neighborhood of Montgomery, known for its historic homes, quaint shops, and local eateries
- The Montgomery Museum of Fine Arts, located just a short drive from the park, offers additional opportunities to explore and appreciate visual arts
- The Alabama Shakespeare Festival, also nearby, presents world-class theatrical productions and educational programs for all ages

Tips for visiting:

- Check the park's website or social media pages for information on current sculptures, programs, and events
- Bring water, snacks, and sun protection, especially during hot summer months, as the park is primarily outdoors
- Encourage children to observe, touch, and interact with the sculptures respectfully, following any posted guidelines or instructions
- Consider bringing art supplies, such as sketchpads or cameras, to document and respond to the park's inspiring installations
- Take advantage of the park's free admission and flexible hours to plan a visit that suits your family's schedule and interests

Bogue's Buddy Art Park is a must-visit destination for families who want to experience the joy, creativity, and educational value of public art in a welcoming and engaging setting. By combining the work of talented local artists with the beauty of the outdoors and the power of imaginative play, the park offers a truly unique and enriching experience that will inspire and delight visitors of all ages. Whether you're a Montgomery resident or a visitor exploring the city's cultural offerings, Bogue's Buddy Art Park promises a memorable and meaningful adventure that celebrates the transformative power of art in our lives and communities.

Marion Splash Park

(Marion)

Address: 3277 Military St S, Marion, AL 36756

Phone: (334) 683-4333

Hours: Seasonal, typically open from late May to early September

Admission: Free

The Marion Splash Park is a wonderful destination for families looking to beat the heat, enjoy outdoor recreation, and create cherished summer memories together. With its interactive water features, safety-focused design, and complementary amenities, the splash park offers a delightful and refreshing experience for visitors of all ages.

Activities and attractions for different age groups:

1. Toddlers and preschoolers (2-5):
    - Splashing and playing in the shallow water areas, which feature gentle sprays and bubblers
    - Exploring the zero-depth entry area, which allows young children to safely enter and exit the water
    - Playing on the nearby playground equipment designed for younger children, such as small slides and climbing structures
2. Elementary school-aged children (6-12):
    - Running through the various water sprayers, fountains, and jets, creating their own aquatic obstacle courses
    - Anticipating and enjoying the periodic deluge

from the giant tipping bucket
  - Engaging in water play with friends and siblings, such as tag or water balloon toss
  - Enjoying picnic lunches or snacks with family in the designated picnic areas
3. Teenagers and adults:
  - Supervising and playing alongside younger children in the splash park area
  - Relaxing in the shaded seating areas or on the grass, enjoying the laughter and excitement of the children at play
  - Capturing photos and videos of the family's splash park adventures to share and treasure
  - Preparing and enjoying picnic meals or snacks in the park's picnic areas

Amenities and accessibility:

- The splash park offers shaded seating areas and benches for visitor comfort and relaxation
- Picnic tables and trash receptacles are available in the adjacent picnic areas
- Restrooms and changing facilities are located nearby for convenient access
- The splash park features a non-slip surface and zero-depth entry area to ensure safety and accessibility for all visitors
- Ample parking is available in the nearby lot, with designated spaces for visitors with disabilities

Safety and comfort: The Marion Splash Park prioritizes the safety and comfort of its visitors through the following features and guidelines:

- The splash park uses a recirculating water system that is regularly monitored and treated to ensure water quality and cleanliness
- The water features are designed with appropriate water pressure and flow to prevent injury or discomfort
- The splash park surface is constructed with a non-slip material to reduce the risk of slips and falls
- Visitors are encouraged to wear water shoes or sandals to protect their feet and improve traction on the wet surfaces
- Parents and caregivers are advised to closely supervise children at all times and ensure they follow splash park rules and guidelines

Nearby attractions and amenities:

- The Marion town square, located just a short walk from the splash park, offers a charming glimpse into the community's history and architecture
- The Perry Lakes Park, located just a short drive from Marion, features hiking trails, fishing lakes, and scenic picnic areas for outdoor enthusiasts
- The Marion Military Institute, a historic military junior college, offers campus tours and cultural events throughout the year
- Various local restaurants, shops, and accommodations are available in the Marion area to cater to visitors' needs and preferences

Tips for visiting:

- Check the splash park's operating hours and season before planning your visit, as they may vary from year to year
- Bring sunscreen, hats, and water shoes to protect your

family from the sun and enhance your splash park experience

- Pack a picnic lunch, snacks, and drinks to enjoy in the park's picnic areas, but be sure to dispose of trash in the provided receptacles
- Encourage children to take breaks, stay hydrated, and use the restroom facilities as needed to ensure a comfortable and enjoyable visit
- Consider combining your splash park visit with other local attractions or activities to create a full day of family fun and adventure

The Marion Splash Park is a must-visit destination for families seeking a fun, refreshing, and memorable summer experience in the heart of Alabama. By offering a variety of interactive water features, prioritizing safety and comfort, and providing complementary amenities, the splash park ensures that visitors of all ages can enjoy a delightful day of outdoor play and relaxation. Whether you're a local resident or a visitor exploring the Marion area, the Marion Splash Park promises a splashing good time that will leave you feeling cool, refreshed, and ready for more family adventures.

Rock City

(Lookout Mountain)

Address: 1400 Patten Rd, Lookout Mountain, GA 30750

Phone: (706) 820-2531

Hours: Hours vary by season

Admission: Adults $26.95, Children (3-12) $15.95, Children under 3 free

Rock City is a magical and awe-inspiring destination that offers families a unique blend of natural beauty, outdoor adventure, and whimsical enchantment. With its stunning rock formations, lush gardens, and educational attractions, Rock City provides an unforgettable experience that will captivate visitors of all ages.

Activities and attractions for different age groups:

1. Toddlers and preschoolers (2-5):
   - Exploring the Fairyland Caverns and Mother Goose Village, which bring beloved fairy tales and nursery rhymes to life through colorful displays and interactive elements
   - Enjoying the park's gentle walking paths and scenic overlooks, which offer plenty of opportunities for imaginative play and discovery
   - Participating in seasonal events, such as the Rocktoberfest or the Enchanted Garden of Lights, which feature kid-friendly activities and decorations
2. Elementary school-aged children (6-12):

- ◦ Navigating the Swing-A-Long Bridge and other adventurous rock formations, which provide a thrilling sense of accomplishment and breathtaking views
- ◦ Learning about the park's geological history and plant life through interactive exhibits and guided tours
- ◦ Engaging in educational scavenger hunts or activity sheets that encourage exploration and learning throughout the park

3. Teenagers and adults:
   - ◦ Marveling at the park's stunning vistas and natural wonders, which offer countless opportunities for photography and scenic appreciation
   - ◦ Challenging themselves on the park's more strenuous hiking trails and rock formations, such as the Needle's Eye and the Fat Man's Squeeze
   - ◦ Enjoying the park's dining options, gift shops, and special events, which provide a welcome respite and a chance to relax and unwind amidst the beauty of nature

Amenities and accessibility:

- Rock City offers several dining options, from quick snacks to full-service restaurants, catering to various tastes and dietary needs
- Gift shops located throughout the park sell souvenirs, apparel, and locally-made crafts
- Restrooms and drinking fountains are available at various points along the trail
- While the park's natural terrain can be challenging, efforts have been made to improve accessibility, with some paved

paths and handrails in certain areas
- Strollers and wheelchairs may be difficult to navigate in some areas due to the park's rocky and uneven surfaces

Special events and experiences: Rock City hosts a variety of special events and experiences throughout the year, such as:

- Seasonal festivals, like the Southern Blooms Festival in the spring or the Rocktoberfest in the fall, which celebrate the changing beauty of the gardens and offer themed activities and entertainment
- The Enchanted Garden of Lights, a dazzling holiday light display that transforms the park into a whimsical winter wonderland
- Outdoor concerts and performances, which take advantage of the park's unique natural setting and acoustics
- Educational programs and workshops, such as birdwatching tours or photography classes, that provide in-depth exploration of the park's natural and artistic wonders

Nearby attractions and accommodations:

- Lookout Mountain offers a variety of other attractions, such as Ruby Falls, the Incline Railway, and the Battles for Chattanooga Museum, which can be combined with a visit to Rock City for a full day of exploration
- Chattanooga, Tennessee, located just a short drive from the park, offers a wide range of dining, shopping, and lodging options, as well as additional cultural and recreational attractions
- The nearby towns of Lookout Mountain and Chattanooga Valley provide a variety of accommodations, from cozy bed and breakfasts to family-friendly hotels, catering to various

budgets and preferences

Tips for visiting:

- Check Rock City's website or social media pages for up-to-date information on hours, ticket prices, and special events, as they may vary seasonally
- Wear comfortable, sturdy shoes with good traction, as the park's trails can be rocky and uneven in places
- Bring a camera to capture the stunning views and memorable moments throughout your visit
- Plan to spend at least 2-3 hours exploring the park, allowing time for both the main trail and the various side attractions and exhibits
- Consider purchasing a combination ticket or package that includes admission to other nearby attractions, such as Ruby Falls or the Incline Railway, for a full day of Lookout Mountain adventures

Rock City is a must-visit destination for families seeking a unique and enchanting outdoor experience that combines natural beauty, adventure, and imagination. With its breathtaking views, whimsical attractions, and educational opportunities, Rock City offers a memorable and enriching experience that will leave visitors of all ages with a sense of wonder and appreciation for the magic of the natural world. Whether you're a local resident or a traveler exploring the region's iconic attractions, Rock City promises an unforgettable journey through a realm where reality and fantasy intertwine, creating a truly one-of-a-kind family adventure.

Alabama Maritime Museum

(Mobile)

Address: 201 E 25th St, Mobile, AL 36615

Phone: (251) 432-1940

Hours: Tuesday-Saturday 9 AM - 4 PM (Closed Sundays and Mondays) Admission: Adults $6, Children (6-17) $3, Children under 6 free

The Alabama Maritime Museum is a fascinating destination that offers families a unique opportunity to explore the rich maritime heritage of Mobile and the Gulf Coast region. With its engaging exhibits, hands-on experiences, and knowledgeable staff, the museum provides an educational and entertaining experience that brings the state's nautical history to life.

Activities and attractions for different age groups:

1. Elementary school-aged children (6-12):
   - Exploring the USS Alabaman, a retired oceanographic survey ship, and discovering the various roles and responsibilities of crew members
   - Participating in interactive exhibits and activities that teach about navigation, knot-tying, and other maritime skills
   - Learning about the diverse marine life of the Gulf Coast through engaging displays and touch tanks
2. Teenagers (13-17):
   - Delving into the history of shipbuilding and maritime trade in Alabama, and understanding their impact on the state's economy and culture

- ○ Discovering the role of the Gulf Coast during times of war and conflict, such as the Civil War and World War II
- ○ Exploring the science and technology behind oceanographic research and maritime navigation

3. Adults:
   - ○ Gaining a deeper appreciation for the challenges and triumphs of life at sea, as well as the importance of maritime industries to the region
   - ○ Learning about the preservation and restoration of historic ships, such as the USS Alabaman
   - ○ Enjoying the museum's temporary exhibits and special events, which highlight specific aspects of maritime history and culture

Amenities and accessibility:

- The museum offers a small gift shop with maritime-themed books, toys, and souvenirs
- Restrooms are available on-site for visitor convenience
- The museum is wheelchair accessible, with ramps and elevators providing access to most areas
- Some areas of the USS Alabaman may have limited accessibility due to the ship's original design and structure

Educational programs and tours: The Alabama Maritime Museum offers a variety of educational programs and tours for families and school groups, including:

- Guided tours of the USS Alabaman and the museum's exhibits, led by knowledgeable docents who share stories and insights about the region's maritime history
- Hands-on workshops and demonstrations that teach

maritime skills and crafts, such as knot-tying, navigation, and boat-building
- School field trip programs that align with state curriculum standards and provide immersive learning experiences for students
- Outreach programs and traveling exhibits that bring the museum's resources and expertise to schools and community centers throughout the region

Nearby attractions and accommodations:

- The museum is located in downtown Mobile, within walking distance of other popular attractions, such as the Gulf Coast Exploreum Science Center and the History Museum of Mobile
- Mobile's historic districts, such as the Dauphin Street and Oakleigh Garden District, offer a variety of dining, shopping, and sightseeing opportunities
- Accommodations in the Mobile area range from budget-friendly hotels to upscale resorts, catering to various preferences and budgets

Tips for visiting:

- Check the museum's website or call ahead for up-to-date information on hours, ticket prices, and special events
- Allow at least 1-2 hours to explore the museum's exhibits and tour the USS Alabaman
- Wear comfortable shoes and clothing, as the museum involves some walking and climbing of stairs
- Consider combining your visit with other nearby attractions, such as the GulfQuest National Maritime Museum or the Mobile Bay Ferry, for a full day of

maritime-themed exploration
- Don't forget to visit the gift shop for unique souvenirs and educational materials to take home

The Alabama Maritime Museum is a hidden gem that provides families with a fascinating glimpse into the rich maritime history and culture of Mobile and the Gulf Coast region. By offering a unique blend of hands-on experiences, engaging exhibits, and educational programs, the museum ensures that visitors of all ages can learn, explore, and appreciate the vital role that the sea has played in shaping Alabama's past and present. Whether you're a history buff, a maritime enthusiast, or simply looking for a fun and educational family outing, the Alabama Maritime Museum promises an unforgettable adventure that will leave you with a deeper understanding and appreciation for the state's coastal heritage.

Alabama Museum of Natural History

(Tuscaloosa)

Address: 427 6th Ave, Tuscaloosa, AL 35401

Phone: (205) 348-7550

Hours: Tuesday-Saturday 10 AM - 4:30 PM (Closed Sundays and Mondays) Admission: Adults $5, Children (3-17) $3, Children under 3 free

The Alabama Museum of Natural History is a must-visit destination for families interested in exploring the fascinating world of natural history and discovering the rich biodiversity and geological wonders of Alabama. With its engaging exhibits, hands-on activities, and knowledgeable staff, the museum provides an educational and entertaining experience that sparks curiosity and fosters a deeper appreciation for the natural world.

Activities and attractions for different age groups:

1. Toddlers and preschoolers (2-5):
    - Exploring the museum's interactive Discovery Room, which features hands-on activities and specimens designed to introduce young children to the wonders of nature
    - Observing live animals, such as turtles and snakes, in the museum's Living Collections exhibits
    - Participating in age-appropriate scavenger hunts or activity sheets that encourage exploration and discovery throughout the museum
2. Elementary school-aged children (6-12):
    - Marveling at the Dinosaur Exhibit, which features

impressive skeletons and fossilized remains of prehistoric creatures
  - Learning about Alabama's diverse ecosystems and wildlife through engaging dioramas and interactive displays
  - Participating in hands-on activities, such as fossil digs or mineral identification, that teach scientific concepts and skills
3. Teenagers and adults:
  - Exploring the museum's extensive collections of rocks, minerals, and fossils, and learning about the geological processes that have shaped Alabama's landscape
  - Gaining a deeper understanding of the state's natural history and the importance of conservation and environmental stewardship
  - Attending special lectures, workshops, or events that highlight current research and discoveries in the fields of paleontology, geology, and biology

Amenities and accessibility:

- The museum offers a gift shop with educational books, toys, and souvenirs related to natural history and science
- Restrooms and water fountains are available on-site for visitor comfort and convenience
- The museum is wheelchair accessible, with ramps and elevators providing access to all exhibit areas
- Some exhibits may have low lighting or tight spaces, which may be challenging for visitors with mobility or sensory issues

Educational programs and tours: The Alabama Museum of Natural History offers a variety of educational programs and tours for families, school groups, and lifelong learners, including:

- Docent-led tours that provide a more in-depth exploration of the museum's exhibits and collections
- School field trip programs that align with state curriculum standards and offer hands-on learning experiences for students
- Summer camps and workshops that provide immersive, multi-day experiences focused on specific topics in natural history and science
- Outreach programs and traveling exhibits that bring the museum's resources and expertise to schools and community centers throughout the state

Research and collections: In addition to its public exhibits, the Alabama Museum of Natural History is also a major research institution, housing extensive scientific collections and conducting ongoing research in the fields of paleontology, geology, and biology. Visitors can learn about the museum's behind-the-scenes work and its contributions to the scientific community through special displays and programs.

Tips for visiting:

- Check the museum's website or call ahead for up-to-date information on hours, ticket prices, and special events
- Allow at least 1-2 hours to explore the museum's exhibits and participate in activities
- Encourage children to ask questions, share observations, and engage with the exhibits to maximize their learning experience

- Consider bringing a camera or sketchbook to document your favorite specimens and displays
- Visit the gift shop for unique souvenirs, educational materials, and gifts that support the museum's mission and programs

The Alabama Museum of Natural History is a hidden gem that offers families a fascinating and educational journey through the state's rich natural heritage. With its combination of impressive exhibits, hands-on activities, and expert-led programs, the museum provides a unique opportunity to discover the wonders of the natural world and gain a deeper appreciation for the incredible diversity and complexity of life on Earth. Whether you're a budding paleontologist, a curious naturalist, or simply a family looking for a fun and educational outing, the Alabama Museum of Natural History promises an unforgettable experience that will leave you inspired and amazed by the marvels of nature.

GatorAlleyFarm.com
Summerdale   AL.

Gator Alley Boardwalk

(Summerdale)

Address: 11175 US-59, Summerdale, AL 36580

Phone: (251) 989-5247

Hours: Daily from 9 AM to 5 PM

Admission: Adults $8, Children (3-12) $5, Children under 3 free

Gator Alley Boardwalk is a fantastic destination for families looking to experience the thrill of observing American alligators in their natural habitat while learning about the importance of wetland conservation. With its engaging wildlife encounters, educational exhibits, and family-friendly amenities, the boardwalk offers a unique and memorable experience for visitors of all ages.

Activities and attractions for different age groups:

1. Toddlers and preschoolers (2-5):
    - Observing alligators from the safety of the boardwalk and learning about their physical characteristics and behavior
    - Exploring the butterfly garden and discovering the colorful world of these delicate insects
    - Enjoying the petting zoo and interacting with friendly animals under adult supervision
2. Elementary school-aged children (6-12):
    - Reading the educational displays and signage along the boardwalk to learn about alligators, wetland ecology, and conservation efforts
    - Participating in guided tours or educational

programs led by knowledgeable staff members
- ◦ Completing scavenger hunts or activity sheets that encourage closer observation and engagement with the exhibits

3. Teenagers and adults:
   - ◦ Photographing alligators and other wildlife from the boardwalk while learning about responsible wildlife viewing practices
   - ◦ Gaining a deeper understanding of the ecological importance of wetlands and the role of alligators within these ecosystems
   - ◦ Supporting conservation efforts through purchases at the gift shop or by making donations to the facility

Amenities and accessibility:

- The boardwalk is wheelchair and stroller accessible, with wide, flat surfaces and sturdy railings for safety
- Restrooms and a small gift shop are available on-site for visitor convenience
- Benches and sheltered areas along the boardwalk provide places to rest and enjoy the surroundings
- Ample parking is available near the boardwalk entrance, with designated spaces for visitors with disabilities

Safety and conservation: Gator Alley Boardwalk prioritizes visitor safety and the well-being of the alligators and other wildlife. Visitors are required to follow a set of guidelines, including:

- Remaining on the boardwalk at all times and not attempting to feed, touch, or disturb the alligators
- Supervising children closely and ensuring they do not

climb on the railings or throw objects into the water

- Respecting the animals and their habitat by not littering or making excessive noise
- Supporting the facility's conservation efforts by learning about the importance of wetland preservation and responsible wildlife interaction

Nearby attractions and accommodations:

- Summerdale is located near the popular beach destinations of Gulf Shores and Orange Beach, which offer a variety of dining, shopping, and lodging options
- Other nearby attractions include the Alabama Gulf Coast Zoo, the Bon Secour National Wildlife Refuge, and the Fort Morgan Historic Site
- Accommodations in the area range from beachfront resorts to charming bed and breakfasts, catering to various budgets and preferences

Tips for visiting:

- Check the weather forecast and dress appropriately for outdoor conditions, with comfortable shoes, sun protection, and insect repellent
- Bring a camera or binoculars to better observe and capture the alligators and other wildlife
- Allow at least 1-2 hours to fully explore the boardwalk and participate in educational activities
- Visit the gift shop for unique souvenirs, educational materials, and items that support the facility's conservation efforts
- Consider combining your visit with other nearby attractions or activities, such as a beach day or a nature

hike, for a full day of family fun

Gator Alley Boardwalk offers families a unique opportunity to safely observe American alligators in their natural habitat while learning about the importance of wetland conservation. By providing a well-maintained boardwalk, educational exhibits, and family-friendly amenities, the facility ensures that visitors of all ages can enjoy a thrilling and informative wildlife experience. Whether you're a nature enthusiast, a budding conservationist, or simply a family looking for an exciting outdoor adventure, Gator Alley Boardwalk promises an unforgettable encounter with some of the Gulf Coast's most iconic and fascinating residents.

Family road trips are a cherished tradition that create lasting memories, but long hours in the car can sometimes lead to boredom and restlessness. To keep everyone entertained and engaged during your journey, we've compiled a list of 25 fun and easy-to-play road trip games suitable for all ages. These games will not only help pass the time but also encourage family bonding, creativity, and friendly competition. Whether you're traveling with toddlers, teens, or a mix of ages, there's something here for everyone. So, buckle up, grab any necessary items, and get ready to enjoy some quality family time on the open road!

Games for All Ages:

I Spy

- Items needed: None
- Instructions: One person starts by saying, "I spy with my little eye, something..." and then describes an object they see. Others take turns guessing until the correct object is identified. The person who guesses correctly takes the next turn.

20 Questions

- Items needed: None
- Instructions: One person thinks of an object, person, or place. The other players take turns asking yes-or-no questions to gather clues. The group has 20 questions to guess the answer.

The Alphabet Game

- Items needed: None

- Instructions: Choose a category (e.g., animals, countries, or foods). Players take turns naming items in the category in alphabetical order. The first player starts with an item beginning with "A," the next player names an item starting with "B," and so on.

The License Plate Game

- Items needed: None
- Instructions: Players try to find license plates from as many different states or countries as possible. The player who spots the most unique license plates wins.

Storytelling

- Items needed: None
- Instructions: One person starts a story with a single sentence. The next player adds another sentence to continue the story. Players take turns adding sentences until the story reaches a natural conclusion.

Games for Younger Children (3-7 years):

Spot the Color

- Items needed: None
- Instructions: Choose a color. Players take turns finding and pointing out objects of that color outside the car. The player who spots the most objects in the chosen color wins.

Rhyme Time

- Items needed: None
- Instructions: One player says a word, and the next player

must say a word that rhymes with it. Continue taking turns until a player cannot think of a rhyme. The last player to say a rhyming word starts the next round with a new word.

Name That Tune

- Items needed: Music playlist
- Instructions: Play a song and pause it after a few seconds. Players take turns guessing the song's title or artist. The first player to guess correctly earns a point.

Car Bingo

- Items needed: Printable car bingo sheets, writing utensils
- Instructions: Before the trip, create bingo sheets with common road trip sights (e.g., a red car, a stop sign, or a cow). Players mark off the items as they spot them. The first player to complete a bingo (horizontal, vertical, or diagonal line) wins.

Counting Cars

- Items needed: None
- Instructions: Choose a color or type of vehicle (e.g., blue cars or trucks). Players count how many of the chosen vehicles they see within a set time limit. The player with the highest count wins.

Games for Older Children and Teens (8+ years):

Would You Rather?

- Items needed: None
- Instructions: One player asks a "Would you rather...?"

question with two choices (e.g., "Would you rather have the ability to fly or be invisible?"). Other players answer and discuss their reasoning.

Two Truths and a Lie

- Items needed: None
- Instructions: Each player takes a turn stating three facts about themselves, with one being a lie. The other players guess which statement is the lie. The player who guesses correctly earns a point.

Geography Challenge

- Items needed: None
- Instructions: One player names a place (e.g., a city, state, or country). The next player must name another place that starts with the last letter of the previous place (e.g., "New York" followed by "Kansas"). Continue until a player cannot think of a new place.

Movie Quote Trivia

- Items needed: None
- Instructions: One player recites a famous movie quote, and the other players try to guess the movie title and/or the character who said it. The first player to guess correctly takes the next turn.

Categories

- Items needed: None
- Instructions: Choose a category (e.g., fruits, sports, or

celebrities). Players take turns naming items in that category without repeating any. If a player repeats an item or cannot think of a new one, they are out. The last player remaining wins.

More Games for All Ages:

Road Trip Scavenger Hunt

- Items needed: Printable scavenger hunt lists, writing utensils
- Instructions: Before the trip, create a list of items players might see during the journey (e.g., a billboard with a specific logo, a certain type of tree, or a particular road sign). Players mark off the items as they spot them. The first player to find all items wins.

Guess the Object

- Items needed: A bag or pillowcase filled with small, common objects
- Instructions: One player secretly selects an object from the bag and describes it without revealing what it is. The other players ask yes-or-no questions to guess the object. The player who guesses correctly selects the next object.

Memory Test

- Items needed: None
- Instructions: One player recites a list of items (e.g., "I went to the store and bought an apple"). The next player repeats the list and adds another item (e.g., "I went to the store and bought an apple and a banana"). Continue taking turns,

with each player reciting the growing list and adding a new item. If a player makes a mistake, they are out.

Guess the Song

- Items needed: Music playlist
- Instructions: One player hums or whistles a tune from a popular song. The other players try to guess the song title and/or artist. The first player to guess correctly hums or whistles the next song.

The Picnic Game

- Items needed: None
- Instructions: The first player says, "I'm going on a picnic, and I'm bringing..." followed by an item that starts with the letter "A" (e.g., "apples"). The next player repeats the phrase, including the first item, and adds a new item starting with "B." Continue through the alphabet, with each player reciting the growing list and adding a new item.

Additional Games for Younger Children:

Animal Guessing Game

- Items needed: None
- Instructions: One player thinks of an animal and gives a clue about its appearance, habitat, or behavior. The other players take turns asking yes-or-no questions to guess the animal. The player who guesses correctly thinks of the next animal.

Silly Faces

- Items needed: None
- Instructions: Players take turns making silly faces at each other. The first player to laugh or smile is out. The last player remaining wins.

Additional Games for Older Children and Teens:

Name That Tune (Humming Edition)

- Items needed: None
- Instructions: One player hums a tune from a popular song. The other players try to guess the song title and/or artist. The first player to guess correctly hums the next song.

Collaborative Storytelling

- Items needed: None
- Instructions: One player starts a story with a single sentence. The next player adds another sentence to continue the story, incorporating a random word or phrase provided by the previous player. Players take turns adding sentences and providing random words or phrases until the story reaches a natural conclusion.

Alphabet Categories

- Items needed: None
- Instructions: Choose a category (e.g., movies, books, or video games). Players take turns naming items in the category in alphabetical order. The first player starts with an item beginning with "A," the next player names an item starting with "B," and so on. If a player cannot think of an item for their letter, they are out.

With these 25 road trip games, your family will be well-equipped to tackle even the longest car rides with enthusiasm and laughter. From classic favorites like "I Spy" and "20 Questions" to creative challenges like "Collaborative Storytelling" and "Alphabet Categories," these games offer a diverse range of activities that cater to different ages and interests. As you play, you'll create shared experiences, inside jokes, and cherished memories that will last long after your road trip ends. So, the next time you hit the highway with your loved ones, remember to pack a few of these games alongside your snacks and suitcases – they'll help make your journey as enjoyable as your destination!

Don't miss out!

Visit the website below and you can sign up to receive emails whenever Discover America Press publishes a new book. There's no charge and no obligation.

https://books2read.com/r/B-A-CJSFB-JIFAD

BOOKS 2 READ

Connecting independent readers to independent writers.

www.ingramcontent.com/pod-product-compliance
Lightning Source LLC
Chambersburg PA
CBHW060901140726
47996CB00001B/65